First Time Parents' Survival Guide

First Time Parents' Survival Guide

Emma Scattergood

Consultant Paediatrician:
Dr Cathy Hill

WARD LOCK

A WARD LOCK BOOK

First published in the UK 1998 by
Ward Lock
Wellington House
125 Strand
London WC2R 0BB

A Cassell Imprint

Distributed in the United States by
Sterling Publishing Co. Inc.
387 Park Avenue South
New York NY 10016-8810

British Library Cataloguing-in-Publication Data

A catalogue record for this book is available from the British Library

ISBN 0–7063–7758–3

Designed by Ben Cracknell Studios
Edited by Harriet Stewart-Jones
Illustrations by Clinton Banbury and Valerie Hill

Printed and bound in Great Britain by Mackays of Chatham

Contents

Acknowledgements

This book could not have been written without the help of the following people: Dr Cathy Hill, consultant in paediatrics, for her medical expertise and friendly support; Annette Connor and Sally Warcup, whose experience as health visitors was invaluable when answering many of the parents' questions; Claire Brookes who was happy to share the details of baby Isaac's first year with us; my husband David, who had to live with a neurotic author; and especially to Lucy and George, my two 'babies' who have provided me with so much first-hand experience, as well as plenty of fun.

Reader's note
We have used 'he' and 'she' in alternate chapters throughout this book to reflect the fact that the text applies equally to female and male babies.

Introduction

Parenting has to be one of the most difficult jobs on earth, but it is also the most rewarding. What other job would expect you to be on call 24 hours a day, make crucial decisions about another human being's health and lifestyle – and sacrifice your own social life, and even your income, in order to do so?

You'll discover sides to you which you never knew existed. You will find that you can survive on less than six hours sleep a night (just); that you can spend a whole day without looking in a mirror, let alone putting on any lipstick; that you have the ability to juggle a telephone, a baby and a drop-cup bra; and that simply sitting and watching your baby can be even more compelling and unmissable than an episode of *Friends*.

The new dad too finds himself completely overwhelmed and amazed at how one little thing can not only wreak such complete havoc on a hitherto relatively sane and ordered household, but also incite such feelings of utter love and fascination. Both of you will also, however, find yourself fretting and worrying over the slightest blemish, hiccup or stage of development in your baby's life – which is where this book comes in.

The *First-time Parents' Survival Guide* will get you through that exciting but trying first year, and give you the advice and support you need to make you both more confident and assured as parents. Based on commonsense advice, rather than the latest trend in parentcraft, the book will take you through every aspect of care from coping with breastfeeding to getting your baby to sleep through the night.

As a new mother myself I would devour every book on babies and parentcraft whenever a problem occurred, but would usually end up throwing each one down with frustration because I could not find the answer I was looking for. In consequence, I have pestered every mother and father I have come across to tell me what their main concerns have been in looking after the new member of the family – and, in particular, which burning questions they have never had properly answered. I then persevered to get all of those problems solved – drawing on my own experience (as a mother of two and writer for parenting magazines), as well as the knowledge of two dedicated health visitors and the expertise of paediatrician Dr Cathy Hill. The results of my quest are published here, and have been combined with tips and ideas from other health visitors, midwives and parents. The result (I hope) is a childcare bible which you will find yourself dipping into for the first year and even beyond.

So, as you start on your new adventure, good luck – and have fun!

1

The first few weeks

Welcome to the world of parenthood! Being a mother or father will be fun, exciting, emotional – and will present its fair share of worry too. In fact these parental anxieties will probably be with you for the next 21 years or more, so get used to the feeling now!

Nothing can really prepare you for the practicalities of looking after a new baby, or the mixed emotions that being a parent can bring. There's no doubt that the first few months can be as tough as they are exciting, but it does get easier. Take only one day at a time and you'll soon look back and realize just how far you've come.

YOUR NEW BABY

The first sight of your baby may not be quite what you were expecting. In general, newborns are not pink, chubby and cherubic. Instead, they may be covered in vernix (the white coating that protected them in the womb), have rather skinny chicken legs, boast a head that looks far too large, and are either completely bald or have hair that looks rather matted and of indeterminate colour until after the first bath. The eyelids may be swollen, and the eyes might even be bloodshot from the exertion of labour – sometimes an ear or two has been flattened in the wrong direction too! If you had an assisted delivery the head may have forceps marks or be temporarily misshapen from the ventouse and, whether you have had a boy or a girl, you may notice that the breasts are somewhat swollen because of the female hormones your baby has been receiving from you.

Of course, despite all this you will think your baby is perfect, and every excited relative who comes to visit will exclaim how beautiful she is, or notice a passing resemblance to a distant aunt. Within a few days you will also notice how much your newborn has changed and how she is already beginning to look far more human!

In the meantime, enjoy counting all her fingers and toes by all means, but don't miss out on this precious time by worrying unduly about your baby's appearance or health – there will be plenty of professionals on hand to do that for you.

My little boy has a bright red birthmark on his upper arm. Will it be permanent and is there anything I can do about it?

Gina, mother to Matthew, eight months old.

A soft, raised strawberry birthmark like this is very common and can sometimes appear suddenly in the first few weeks of life, starting as a purple flat mark. It may grow for a while but will fade and disappear by the time your child is ten years old, and usually by school age. Until then it is best left alone unless it continues to grow. It may bleed occasionally, especially if it is scratched or bumped, but just apply some pressure to stem the flow.

THE FIRST PRIORITIES

Once your baby has been given an initial clean and check by the midwife and she is happy that all is well, she'll be handed back to you and you can begin to get to know each other. If you had a hospital delivery, your baby will be given a little cot at your bedside and that will be the centre of your world for the next day or so. In hospital you can relax in the knowledge that you are surrounded by experienced hands, you do not have to worry about food or housework, and you can devote all your time to learning about your new baby and how to care for her.

Don't be scared to lift and cuddle your baby – she's much tougher than she looks and in fact will prefer to be handled firmly (but gently) as it will make her feel more secure. Whenever you get the chance, have a skin-to-skin cuddle – your baby will learn to recognize your smell and it will help you to develop a special bond. Research has repeatedly shown that the more physical contact babies have, the more healthy and happy they become – so go for it!

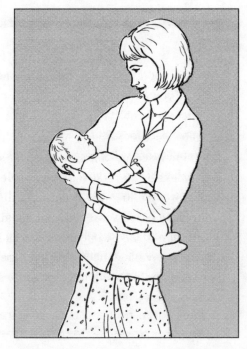

When you lift your newborn baby, first slip one hand under her neck and head for support and slide your other arm beneath her back. Cradle her head in the crook of your elbow and support her bottom with your hand, holding her close to your body. Babies take several weeks to develop neck muscles strong

Q

My baby cries when I hold him on his back like I see all the other babies being carried. I don't know what I'm doing wrong.

Marion, mother to Tom, three days old.

All babies have different preferences. Perhaps Tom would simply prefer to be in a more upright position. Keep one hand under his head and neck and the other under his buttocks while you lift him up to shoulder level. As babies become more interested in the world, many like to be upright so that they can see what is going on over your shoulder. You could try carrying him with his back to your chest, holding him snugly with one arm against his chest and the other under his bottom so that he can see in front of you.

enough to support their own heads so you need to protect her head until then. If you want to put her down, bring her body down first then support her head until it touches the mattress too. Always put her down on her back for safety.

Your confidence will soon grow and before long you will find yourself naturally rocking your baby – in fact you'll discover maternal instincts you never knew you had!

Even if your baby is premature, it is important that you touch and handle her (if your doctors allow it). Although she may look terribly frail, studies have shown that premature babies who are stroked and touched while in intensive care can benefit – and you will feel better for doing it too. To begin with you may only be able to touch her through the portholes of an incubator, but soon you will be able to take her out for a proper cuddle.

NAPPIES – AND THEIR CONTENTS

Changing nappies is not the big deal that many new fathers make it out to be, whether you've decided to go for disposables, terry towelling or shaped reusable nappies. If you are still undecided about which sort of nappy to use, you may want to use disposables for the first few weeks while the nappy changes are more frequent and, in the early days, more sticky! Then, once you've got more of an idea about what you are dealing with, you can make a considered decision about which nappies will suit you and your lifestyle, as well as suiting the environment.

For the first day or so, your baby will be excreting sticky greenish black meconium which is hellish to get off a little bottom and even worse to get off the bedclothes. Luckily, it doesn't last for long and you know that once you've mastered that, you are prepared for anything that your baby presents you with in the nappy department. The bowel movements for the next three days or so will be bright yellow and very loose, with a seedy texture. Thereafter what your baby produces will depend very much on what goes in the other end. Breastfed babies present a very loose (sometimes watery) golden yellow movement, reminiscent of wholegrain mustard, whereas formula-fed babies will fill their nappies with something more solid and anything from pale yellow to brown in colour. They also, unfortunately, tend to pong a bit more than the nappies produced by breastfeeders.

As long as your baby is wetting her nappy frequently and filling it with something more substantial most days, you can be confident that everything down below is in working order.

CHANGING A NAPPY

As a general rule, you'll need to change your baby's nappy when she wakes up in the morning, after every feed and before she goes to bed at night – so that's probably going to be about seven times a day in the early weeks. You'll also need to clean your baby's bottom at every nappy change to help to prevent soreness. A newborn's skin is very sensitive so it's best to wash it using water and cottonwool rather than baby wipes at first, but after a few months you may find it more convenient to switch to wipes.

   Before you start, make sure that you have everything you need close to hand so that you don't have to leave your baby halfway through. Your mental checklist should include:

- ✿ a changing mat
- ✿ warm water
- ✿ cottonwool
- ✿ tissue paper
- ✿ nappy cream
- ✿ a clean nappy
- ✿ a nappy sack or a bin for disposing of dirty nappies.

Lie your baby down on the changing mat and take off the dirty nappy. Use the inside front of the nappy followed by tissue paper to remove any faeces from her bottom. Then dampen a piece of cottonwool and clean her bottom thoroughly, going into all the creases.

As soon as my baby learnt to turn over she would never stay still for a
nappy change. I've found it helpful to change her under a mobile or
activity arch and with a stack of different toys to hand so that I can
keep her interested in something while she lies on her back.

Zoe, mother to Courtney, seven months old.

Lift her legs up out of the way with one hand, keeping a finger between
the two ankles to prevent them rubbing together. Always clean your
baby's bottom from front to back to prevent germs reaching the vagina
and never pull back the labia to clean inside. For boys, never try to pull
back the foreskin to clean under it.

Dry your baby's bottom thoroughly with a tissue. It is helpful to let
her kick for a while with her nappy off to make sure the nappy area is
completely dry – you can always put a towel under her in case she
decides to perform again. Airing the bottom for a while each day helps
to prevent nappy rash – and cure it too.

As disposable nappies are now so efficient at absorbing moisture
there is no need to use a barrier cream on your baby's bottom all the
time, but keep a pot of medicated cream for the times when it looks a
little pink and sore. If you use terry nappies, a barrier cream, such as
petroleum jelly, will protect your baby's skin from the urine.

Once your baby is clean and dry and ready for a clean nappy, the
technique for putting it on will depend on the type you use:

Disposable nappies   Open up the nappy and slip it under your baby's
bottom so that the tabs are at the top behind her. Bring the bottom
half up between her legs and smooth the side panels around her
tummy so that they tuck in neatly. Unpeel the tabs and fasten them
at the front so that the nappy is snug but not too tight. Repeat on
the other side. If you have used cream, make sure that you don't get
any on the tabs – this is a common cause of failure for the

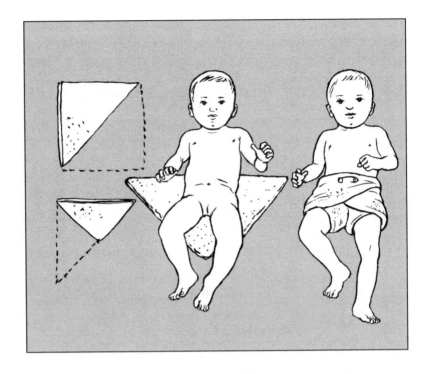

inexperienced nappy changer. Don't despair if you don't get it right first time – the joy of most new disposable nappies is that the tabs can be repositioned if you muck it up!

Terry nappies   Lie the nappy square in front of you, then fold it into a triangle by lifting the bottom right-hand corner to the opposite corner, then the bottom left corner to the top right. Slide it under your baby's bottom so that the top is level with her waist. Bring the nappy up between her legs and fold over the two sides, one at a time towards the centre, pulling slightly to keep the nappy snug. Fasten it at the front with a nappy pin. As your baby grows, you'll need to use two pins, one at each side.

Shaped terry nappies   These fasten like disposables, with Velcro tabs.

> Every now and then my baby presents us with a nappy that is so awful
> we can't do anything but wipe off the worst with tissue and pop her in
> the bath to clean her. We've even had to do it at friends' houses now
> and then!
>
> Sarah, mother to Emily, six months old.

DISPOSING OF NAPPIES

You could keep a pedal bin lined with a plastic sack in the baby's room
especially for nappies and empty it daily into your outside bin –
although dirty nappies can smell a bit too offensive to leave around for
very long. Otherwise you can buy the packs of scented nappy sacks and
dispose of the nappies individually. Also look out for the specially
designed pedal bins which contain a roll of nappy sack plastic. Each
time you put a nappy in the bin you twist the lid to automatically seal
the sack. The bin holds at least a day's supply of nappies hygienically
and without much 'pong', so you are saved from making frequent trips
to the outside bin.

WASHING NAPPIES

Fill two buckets with water and sterilizing solution – one for the soiled
nappies (flush the excess faeces down the toilet first though) and one
for the nappies that are just wet. Keep the nappies in there overnight
then wash the soiled ones in the washing machine. The urine-soaked
ones can simply be rinsed and dried.

The alternative is to cheat and use a nappy washing service. These
are springing up everywhere now and will even come and pick up your
dirty nappies for you and return them fresh and clean.

KEEPING YOUR BABY CLEAN

BATHTIME

The combination of a wriggly baby and a tub of water can seem very daunting to nervous new parents, but don't worry. Your baby doesn't need to be bathed every day at first, and by the time she is crawling around and getting rather grubby, you'll be very much more relaxed about the whole thing. The hospital staff or community midwife will probably help you the first time, or you could always ask an experienced friend (or your mother) to give you a hand.

> In the first few days at home I felt more confident bathing my baby in the hand basin, with flannels wrapped around the taps so he couldn't hurt himself. It felt more contained and I'm sure he felt more secure.
>
> Claire, mother to Joe, three months old.

Before you start, you will need to set up:

- ✿ a warm room (at least 20°C/68°F)
- ✿ a baby bath half filled with warm water (check it with your elbow)
- ✿ a soft towel
- ✿ a changing mat
- ✿ a change of clothes and nappy
- ✿ liquid baby soap and shampoo.

Pick up your baby so that her shoulders and neck are supported on your forearm and her bottom is held by your other hand. Lower her into the bath slowly, smiling at her and talking gently to her all the time so that she feels secure. You can take away the hand that was under her bottom, but continue to support her neck and head in your other hand.

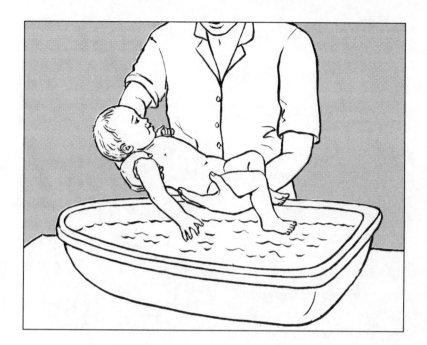

Gently splash the water over her body for a few minutes and rub a little baby shampoo into her hair if necessary. Rinse it by splashing the water over head, but not so that it goes into her eyes. (Some people find it easier to wash a baby's hair when she is not in the bath, but being held above it wrapped in a towel.)

Lift your baby out after a few minutes and wrap her up in a towel before she gets cold. When you dry her, be sure to dry her many little creases. You shouldn't need to use baby powder or lotion – in fact the less products you use on a baby's new, sensitive skin, the better.

When my baby began to outgrow his baby bath I put it into our big bathtub while I bathed him for a few evenings. It helped him get used to the new space and he wasn't at all worried when it came to leaving his little bath behind.

Maggie, mother to Anderson, eight months old.

TOPPING AND TAILING

On the days when your baby doesn't
need a bath, you can give her a
thorough wash instead, using
cooled boiled water at a
handwarm temperature and
cottonwool. Some babies
prefer this as they can stay in
their vest instead of being
stripped bare.

Dip the cottonwool in
the water and clean your
baby's face and neck, paying
particular attention to the
creases under the chin where old
milk and dribble tends to hide! Use a
different piece of cottonwool for each eye in
case there is any infection present, and dry her face with tissue
or a soft towel.

Uncurl your baby's hands and wipe the fingers and palms clean
then dry them with a towel. If she won't open them, try stroking the
back of her hand – in the early weeks the reflex palmar release will
make her oblige.

Next take off her nappy and give her bottom a thorough wash, as
described above in the section on Changing a nappy (page 13).

THE UMBILICAL CORD STUMP

Caring for the remains of the umbilical cord until it comes off is
something that fills many parents with dread, as it can look so delicate.
However it's important that you do clean it daily or it may become

infected. Cooled boiled water should be enough to keep it clean, but make sure you allow it to dry properly before you put a nappy on and keep an eye out for any redness or discharge. Turn down the top of the nappy so that it does not rub against the navel, and expose it to the fresh air as much as possible. It should shrivel up and drop off naturally at around five to ten days after the birth. Continue bathing the area gently at bathtimes afterwards.

Sometimes the area around a baby's tummy button can become quite swollen and protrude noticeably – especially if she is straining. This is nothing to do with your handling of the cord stump, but is what is known as an umbilical hernia. Although it sounds serious, an umbilical hernia is nothing to worry about and should not require any treatment. It happens when the opening which allowed your baby's blood vessels to extend into the umbilical cord doesn't close completely, allowing a small bit of the intestine to bulge through and push up the umbilicus and surrounding area. The swelling will gradually get smaller as the opening closes within a few months or at the latest by the time your baby is two years old.

Q ━━━━━━━━━━━━━━━━━━━━━━━

After my baby's cord stump fell off she was left with a pinky knub of flesh. What can I do about it?

Cathy, mother to Emily, two weeks old.

Show your doctor or health visitor. This is quite a common occurrence known as umbilical granuloma and treating the area with a silver nitrate stick will help to cauterize the area so it heals.

━━━━━━━━━━━━━━━━━━━━━━

FINGERNAILS

Babies are sometimes born with long fingernails which can cause problems if they scratch themselves, particularly on the face. It is best to avoid cutting them with scissors as you may cut the skin by accident. Babies' nails are very soft and it is often possible to simply bend the excess length down and tear it off gently. Some mothers swear that nibbling the nails is the best way. An alternative is to use special small baby nail clippers and to wait until your baby is asleep before attempting to use them. I am not a fan of scratch mittens (unless a baby has bad eczema) as they prevent your baby from discovering her hands and putting them in her mouth.

IT'S TWINS

As soon as you discover that you are having twins you feel different to other pregnant women. You are a different shape, have different expectations and are likely to have a different sort of birth. Sometimes being different makes you feel special, but there are also bound to be plenty of occasions when you wish you were more like everyone else and didn't have to buy two of everything in the nursery departments, try to feed two babies at once and cope with two babies when they cry. Having twins *is* different and it *is* special, but every new parent has to learn a completely new set of skills when their baby is born – you just have to learn a slightly different way of coping.

The one essential the new parents of twins need is dedicated information – but that, unfortunately, can be hard to find. The best source is likely to be people who are already parents to twins and are happy to share their tips and offer support. Track down a twins network to join (see Useful contacts, page 172) or, if there isn't one near you, try advertising for other parents to come forward, via the noticeboard at your doctor's surgery, the hospital or your health visitor. Be careful though that you do not end up socializing purely with other families with twins – your children need to mix with singletons too!

The first few months will inevitably be the hardest – they are for any new parents – but they are especially so when you have double trouble. Whenever your partner is at home you can share the chores and the childcare, but make sure that you do not fall into the habit of taking a certain baby every time – the babies need to get to know you both, equally.

Many new parents find it helpful to keep a record book of what time the baby fed, on what side (if breastfeeding) and for how long, etc. For twins this sort of note-taking is practically an essential if you want some sort of control over your life. A new parent's brain, deprived of sleep, is rarely at its sharpest so a hard record will prevent agonizing mind-searching and domestic rows. Note down who fed well, who did not, who has been bathed, who slept when. Also make a note of which one contracted any significant illness. Although it is likely that both will catch anything that is going, there may be the odd time that they do not.

Whenever you get the chance, care for both your babies at the same time – it halves the time and almost the effort for you, and they will enjoy it too. Bath them together, take them for a walk in a double buggy and play with them together. If you also wake them up and put them to sleep at the same time they will settle into a similar routine more quickly.

WHAT ABOUT YOU?

It's easy for family and friends, and even for you and your partner, to be so excited about the new arrival that you forget that you have actually been through quite a tough time and are in need of some tender loving care yourself. After all, it's not called labour for nothing!

How you feel in the immediate days after the birth will depend very much on how it went. If you needed an episiotomy you'll be rather tender down below and if you had a caesarean it will be several days before you are moving more comfortably. Even if the delivery was completely straightforward, you will still need to take it easy for a few days, however tempting it is to jump up to greet visitors and arrange your flowers. You need to regain your strength and prepare yourself for the interrupted nights that lie ahead, so catch 40 winks whenever you get the chance, even if that means telling enthusiastic visitors to come another day. If you are staying in hospital after the birth, the hospital's own routine should encourage you to rest as much as possible and limit your visitors, but if you are at home, you or your partner will need to be strict with yourselves.

YOUR STRANGE NEW BODY

Don't worry if, at the moment, your body seems quite unlike your own – either the pregnant version or the one you distantly remember having before then. The baby may have gone, but that doesn't mean you will immediately snap back into shape – you will probably be wearing some of your maternity clothes or your more comfy elasticized skirts and trousers for a few weeks more.

Forget faddy diets
This is not the time for dieting, especially if you are breastfeeding. Breastfeeding in itself uses at least an extra 600 calories a day and you

need to have a healthy diet in order to provide your baby with a good supply of milk. Many women find that they can eat what they like when they are breastfeeding and still lose weight, whereas others find it easier to shed the extra pounds after they have stopped feeding their baby themselves. Either way, for the sake of you and your baby, you should make sure you are having three good meals a day, and the odd healthy snack in between, or perhaps five light meals a day, if that's what you prefer.

If you ate quite sensibly when you were pregnant and put on no more than 10–15kg (20–30lb), you should find that you naturally lose any surplus, without dieting, within two or three months after having your baby. If you do have a bit more to lose, sticking to a sensible diet now and taking regular exercise with the pram will help you to quickly wave goodbye to the extra pounds.

Toning up
A lot of the extra flesh you can see around your tummy is not the result of overeating. For the first few days after delivery you will still be carrying nearly 2kg (5lb) of excess fluid, which will naturally flush itself out within a week or so. (You may find you perspire a lot in the first few days and especially at night, as a result.) Your uterus is also still enlarged which will make your tummy look rather pregnant in shape until it has fully contracted to its pre-pregnancy state and slipped back into the pelvis. The sharp afterpains, like contractions, which you experience a day or so after delivering your baby are helping your uterus to do this and the process is normally completed by the time your baby is six weeks old. (Don't worry, the afterpains only last a week at most!)

What you can do something about, however, is your stretched abdominal muscles. Time alone will not get these muscles back to their pre-pregnancy state – sadly, they do need a little help from you. As long as you didn't have a caesarean, there's no reason why you can't start to do a few gentle abdominal exercises as soon as three days after the birth. If you had a surgical delivery, then you will have to wait until after your six-week check and talk to your doctor about starting exercise again.

In most hospitals a physiotherapist will hand out a sheet of exercises for new mothers to follow during their hospital stay. If you don't get one of these you could ask your health visitor or doctor for details. Some of the exercises you can try include the following:

Pelvic tilt   Lie on your back with your arms at your side, your knees raised, and your feet apart. Try to press the small of your back flat into the floor as you inhale, then exhale and relax, allowing your back to return to its normal position. Repeat this three or four times to start with, gradually increasing the number you do.

Head lift   Once you have mastered the pelvic tilt, you can add a head raise. In the same position as before, raise your head as you inhale. Only raise your head as far as it will go without your stomach muscles bulging upwards and keep your shoulders on the floor. Repeat three or four times, increasing gradually.

Sit-up   Once you are comfortable with this you can do a full sit-up, lifting your shoulders off the ground as well, but again, only as far as you can go without your stomach muscles bulging.

RECOVERING FROM A CAESAREAN

If you had a caesarean you need to give yourself a chance to recover from what is, essentially, an operation, as well as coping with the other discomforts of being a new mother. Your scar will be painful, you may be feeling sick from an anaesthetic, suffering from painful wind and you won't be feeling very mobile. Hospital staff will encourage you to at least wriggle your toes to start with and then to get out of bed. You may think they are determined to finish you off completely, but it really is in your best interests to get mobile as it will improve your circulation, reduce the chance of developing a blood clot and will help you feel better more quickly.

You won't be allowed to lift your baby initially, but you can hold her and cuddle her and feed her as normal with the help of some pillows for support. Ask the staff for as much help as you need and keep them informed about any physical discomfort you have, as they will be able to offer you appropriate drugs to relieve the symptoms.

As soon as the dressing is removed from your scar, take a good look at it. It's important that you know what it should look like so that you can recognize any changes. You will need to report any swelling, redness or oozing to your doctor.

When you go home you won't be able to cope with stairs very well. You may have to adapt your home temporarily so that you have everything you need downstairs and don't have to make trips up and down during the day. You also won't be allowed to drive or do any heavy lifting for six weeks after the birth so you will need to arrange someone to do any housework and shopping.

BLOOD LOSS

All women have to put up with some blood loss, or lochia, after giving birth, though many are surprised at how much there is to begin with and how long it can continue. For the first few days it can be quite heavy and there may be an increased gush if you get up suddenly. After three or four days it normally slows and turns from bright red to watery pink, then brown and finally to a yellowy white. In total it may last anything from two to six weeks.

It is not a good idea to use tampons so stock up instead with special maternity sanitary towels or night-time towels – many a flustered man has been despatched to the chemist when the required supply has been underestimated! Sometimes you will think that the flow is finally subsiding only to be disappointed the following day, especially if you are suddenly more active. If the actual bleeding goes then starts again it could be a sign that you are doing too much and need to slow down. Listen to your body.

If you are still actually bleeding after a couple of weeks tell your midwife or doctor as you may have retained a small bit of placenta or your uterus may not have healed properly where the placenta was once attached.

Rarely, a new mother will have a sudden haemorrhage – a rush of blood quite unlike the gradual flow of lochia, 7–14 days after the birth. If this happens to you, it is vital that you contact your doctor immediately or go to hospital, lying down as much as you can in the meantime. A post-partum haemorrhage can be the result of a variety of factors. Usually it is because you have retained a small part of your placenta, but it may be because the uterus has been 'overworked' by a traumatic delivery or a multiple birth – or because you were weakened at the birth due to a general anaesthetic. You may need a blood transfusion and have to be put under anaesthetic to have any retained placenta removed.

CARING FOR STITCHES

If you needed stitches after the delivery you will be feeling particularly sore down below, especially when you sit down. You can take pain-relieving drugs even if you are breastfeeding so there's no need to suffer unnecessarily, but you will still feel as if you are taking a walk after a long horse ride. Movement is good for recovery, so don't sit in one position for long. Sitting on a rubber ring or a pack of frozen peas are both said to make the times you do have to spend in your armchair a little bit more comfortable, but remember to mark the peas you use accordingly so you don't serve them up to your mother-in-law for dinner at a later date.

You will probably find the area stings at first when you pass water. To help this try rinsing your stitches afterwards using a jug of clean water or a bidet – or try standing astride the toilet so that the flow doesn't run past the sensitive area. Some people also find it helpful to hold a pad against their stitches when they make a bowel movement as it makes them feel more secure. Drinking plenty of fluids and eating more fruit than usual so that you don't get constipated makes the whole business much easier.

BEATING THE BABY BLUES

It is quite common to feel weepy and depressed a few days after your baby has arrived – so common in fact that it has been given its own term, the 'baby blues'. This time tends to coincide with your milk coming in (giving you breasts like torpedoes) and the drop in your oestrogen and progesterone levels, and usually only lasts a few days – although some women find that it comes and goes over the first couple of months. Of course it is easy to attribute everything to

If I had suffered any sort of depression immediately after the birth I think I would have recognized it as the baby blues. Instead I had an attack of the blues after I stopped breastfeeding when Lucas was four months old. I felt everything was going wrong, my work, my marriage, the lot. I felt completely inadequate. I never considered that my hormone levels must be all over the place at that time and no one ever told me that I was vulnerable then. As it was, I felt better within about 12 weeks, but it would have been easier if I'd known why I felt like that in the first place.

Jane, mother to Lucas, eight months old.

your hormones at this time, and there may be other quite valid reasons for you feeling down and tearful, such as a fear of leaving hospital to go home (or, conversely, a frustration at being stuck in hospital); a sense of anticlimax now your pregnancy has ended; sheer exhaustion and lack of sleep; disappointment with the way the labour went or your appearance now; worry about your abilities as a mother; and physical discomfort.

I really feel 'cheated' out of a proper birth, because I had a caesarean. I know that I should just be grateful that I've got a healthy baby, but I can't help feeling this way and getting depressed about it.

Catriona, mother to Stephane, one week old.

Many women feel 'cheated' out of a normal birth following a caesarean section. Your visions of what the birth would be like have not been realized and you may feel that control has been taken out of your hands. On top of that you have to cope with a new baby while recovering from surgey and a general anaesthetic. Many women in your position find they get depressed. What you need is a good listener who will allow you to talk openly about your experience and your concerns. This may be a relative, a friend or a professional such as a health visitor, but there are also, in many areas, groups of women who have gone through a similar experience and who meet regularly for support and encouragement. Ask your health visitor about this.

If you are worried or upset about something in particular then see what you might do to rectify the situation. Talk it over with your partner, but try not to overanalyse your feelings as that in itself can contribute to your blues. Sometimes you have to accept that you feel a little bit down at the moment, but given time and some sleep you will feel better.

There are certain circumstances though when you do need to seek professional help. If you feel out of control, are worried that you might hurt yourself or your baby, or have a persistent depression and feeling of hopelessness, you should talk to your doctor and seek help. Various organizations exist to provide advice and support for women in this situation (see Useful contacts, page 172). About 10 per cent of mothers suffer not from baby blues, but a more serious postnatal depression and need counselling and treatment. No one will think any worse of you for admitting that you need help.

THE FIRST FEW DAYS AT HOME

Following a hospital birth, some women cannot wait to get their baby home and start a 'proper' life as a family, but others are reluctant to make the move and are worried that they will not cope at home, away from the support of the hospital environment and staff. If you are concerned, the important thing to realize is that you will never be completely alone if you do not want to be. If you need to talk to anyone or ask for advice, your health visitor and the community midwives will be on hand. Your doctor is there any time you or the baby is ill and there are plenty of support groups for mothers at home. You just need to pick up the phone.

Hopefully your partner will be able to be at home to help you out for the first few days of adjustment. There will be plenty to do in terms of unpacking from hospital, receiving gifts, flowers and visitors, making numerous cups of tea and, oh yes, looking after the new baby! If your partner needs to go back to work, arrange for your mother or a friend to stay or pop in regularly if you want it. It is helpful to have someone to hand the baby to when you want a rest and to have someone around who does not expect to be entertained. If you don't have that sort of help available then could you pay for some? Looking after the baby might seem much more manageable if you have someone to do the housework for example. There are even people known as doulas who can be hired to help both mother and baby in the early days (contact Birth and Bonding International, 01773 826055).

BE EASY ON YOURSELF

In the early days at home with your baby, do not even think about trying to set up a routine – it will be too chaotic! Your baby will probably wake up, feed and sleep at different times each day and it will be up to you to snatch opportunities for getting dressed, having a nap, eating lunch and so on. Go with the flow and let your baby lead the way for now. If you wake up each morning with 101 plans for the day, you'll only go to bed disappointed. If you are the sort of person who is keen to have achieved something positive every day, then make it simple, such as 'Today I'll give her a bath' or 'If the weather's nice, we'll go for a walk'. You never know, you might manage that!

I'm a doctor who cares for babies for a living, but when it came to having my own, I went to pieces. I was really worried that I wouldn't be able to cope at home and I wanted to stay in hospital for as long as I could. They had to practically drag me out! In fact when I got home I found it was easier, and so much quieter than being in hospital.

Rowena, mother to Tom, ten months old.

Your house is bound to be a chaotic mix of nappies, equipment, flowers, gifts, visitors and midwives for the first week or so. Your bed will probably never get made, the washing will mount up and the vacuum cleaner will rest undisturbed in the understairs cupboard – but that's absolutely fine. You can worry about dust in a few weeks time. The important thing is to give you and your baby time to rest, feed and get to know each other. Hopefully your partner will make himself useful with the cooking and other basic chores – if not, try dropping a few broad hints. Another good technique is to stay in your dressing gown for the first few days. You probably won't get much of a chance to dress yourself anyway, but pottering around in your robe will be a reminder to you, your partner and your visitors that you are still 'recovering' and in need of rest.

Q

I know that my wife is having a hard time at home with the baby, but I feel that I come home at the worst possible time when everyone is tired and cranky. We never seem to talk like we used to and, although I know that sex is probably off the agenda for a while, she heads off to bed so early that we don't even have a cuddle before she's asleep.

Jon, father to Helen, eight weeks old.

It is hard being a father for the first time, but being aware of your wife's extra workload is a good start. By the time many men get home in the evening, new mothers (and their babies) are often at their lowest ebb. Not only is your wife physically tired, but she may feel she has accomplished little. Her self-esteem may be very low.

Your great asset is to be able to come into this situation fresh and free to help. If you cook dinner, tidy up or look after the baby while she has a break, she will feel less pressurized.

Sex will return at some point. For some couples it takes weeks, for others it is more a matter of months, but in the meantime undemanding contact is good for you both. Express your love by giving her small gifts or love notes, touching or stroking her and giving her verbal reassurance and encouragement. Remember that you may think that she's doing brilliantly, but she may feel inadequate, disillusioned and disorganized. If you can help her to feel loved and valued I can almost guarantee you will soon find life improving.

Q

I am really keen to get my baby into a routine so that he knows it's bedtime and settles down properly, but I don't even know when his bedtime is because he feeds every three hours.

Collette, mother to Robbie, ten days old.

A bedtime routine is important (see the chapter on Sleep), but it will make little difference when your baby is only ten days old. In fact you may only find you are tying yourself into knots trying to stick to it. Your baby will almost certainly settle down over the next few weeks and by the time he is two or three months old it may be a bit clearer when he is winding down for a longer sleep in the evening.

If you do feel ready to start a routine then, choose a 'bedtime' that would suit you all eventually, say 7.30 pm, and get into the habit of giving him a bath and putting on his pyjamas so that he is ready for bed then. Of course he may wake up for a feed three hours later, but treat that as a night-time feed and keep the lights low and noise to a minimum. He'll soon get the idea.

Survival tips

Don't be worried if your baby does not look like a little
cherub straight away – she soon will.

Changing a nappy may seem to take hours for the first week
or so, but by the end of the month you will be completing
the whole job in five minutes flat – and taking two phone
calls at the same time!

Bathtimes should be fun for both of you. If it isn't, go for a
dry land approach to cleanliness instead.

New mothers should avoid full-length mirrors for the first
six weeks at least – and do not think about trying on your
old jeans for another six weeks after that.

The only diet you should be on is a healthy one. You need
all the energy you can get for now.

If anyone tut-tuts about the dust building up in
your home, just hand them a duster. You have
more important things to worry about.

2

Sleep

Having a baby who sleeps well at night is something most new parents dream of (or would, if they were asleep for long enough). We grown-ups need our sleep – ideally seven or eight uninterrupted hours. Without it we become grouchy and miserable and find coping with normal day-to-day living (let alone the exhausting demands of a young baby) very hard indeed. Unfortunately a young baby just doesn't understand that. He is born with no idea about what is night, what is day and why we like to close everything down at roughly the same time every night. He has to learn to adapt to our way of doing things and, for some babies, that can take a little while.

In the early weeks however, you really can expect very little of your baby. He's not only very new to this world, he has a very tiny stomach that needs to be kept comfortably full. This means constant topping up with milk, round the clock, maybe as often as every three hours or more to start with. So don't expect to get much in the way of uninterrupted sleep for the first six weeks at least.

It is easy to become obsessed with sleep (or rather, your lack of it) during this time, and you will wonder if life will ever be the same again – but don't worry, it will get better. With a bit of luck and maybe some guidance, in a few months you'll wake up after a full night's sleep, wondering what on earth has happened!

THE BASICS

WHERE YOUR BABY SHOULD SLEEP

Where your baby sleeps is very much a personal decision, but in making it, you may want to be guided by the following issues:

- ✿ The health of your baby (more particularly the risk of cot death and protection from cigarette smoke).
- ✿ Practicality (based on matters of space, comfort and what will provide everyone with the best night's sleep).
- ✿ What you will want in the future (some privacy in your own bed for example).

Although it is yet to be proven, some researchers examining the causes of sudden infant death syndrome (SIDS) or cot death have suggested that babies who sleep in the same room as their parents are less at risk of cot death than those who sleep in another room. With this in mind, it may be advisable to have the cot or crib in your bedroom for the first six months of your baby's life, after which time the risk of cot death is significantly reduced. There are other good reasons for having the baby in your room for this period of time – namely, convenience. For the first three months you will be up at least once in the night to feed your baby. If he is down the other end of a draughty corridor then you will find the whole process of getting up to feed far more disruptive to your sleep than if you just have to reach over to a crib at the side of your bed. And, if you don't hear him until his cries have reached fever pitch, then he will be that much harder to settle for a feed and take longer to go back to sleep again afterwards.

So why not have the baby in bed with you? This is a debate that raises strong arguments for both sides. There are many individuals and cultures that advocate sharing a bed with your baby as a way of bonding and ensuring that your baby feels warm, loved and reassured.

However, there are others who argue that once you let a baby into bed with you he will never be out of it. They paint a picture of you, your partner and your children spending the rest of your life crowded into one bed as a result – so that your chances of an exciting sex life will never be the same again, let alone the likelihood of a good night's sleep. Whether or not you let your baby sleep with you really comes down to personal preference, but perhaps the deciding factor should be your baby's safety. In the past the party line has been that, unless you are drunk or drugged, your baby will come to no harm in bed with you, but some further research into cot death has suggested that a baby may be safer in his own bed as he is less likely to overheat there. Babies who spend the whole night in the same bed as their parents do seem to be at higher risk from cot death.

My view is that, as long as you respond to your baby's cry promptly, he is going to feel no less loved for being a few inches from your bed and in fact having him in a crib of his own may help you all get a better night's sleep. However, I also think a little bit of flexibility is called for. There will be times, especially in the first few weeks, when it seems the only solution to a bad night is to take your baby into bed with you. If that is the case, fine. Don't worry that it will be the end of your strict bedtime regime forever, and you are setting a pattern for disaster – you and your baby are both human after all, and following your instinct is often better than adhering to a set of rules.

WHAT SORT OF BED TO CHOOSE

This comes down to a matter of budget as much as anything else. As long as a baby is safe, warm and comfortable, he really will not care whether he sleeps in a crib adorned with frills or a simple wooden drawer – it is the parents who appreciate the trimmings. Basically, for the first 12 weeks, you can choose between using a carrycot, a Moses basket or a rocking crib.

Carrycot   This has the advantage of doubling up as a pram during the day, making it more cost effective, and it can be carried about the house as needed, although it may be a little heavy. You can also transport a baby in the car in a carrycot, as long as you buy a proper restraint for it.

Moses basket   This looks very pretty and is lightweight, which makes it handy for carrying around the house with you. However, it can be a rather expensive item, considering it will only last 12 weeks at the most. You may also want to buy a stand for it, unless you have a piece of furniture you can rest it on at night.

Rocking crib This is another very attractive item, and will last through generations if necessary, but its use per baby is limited as it won't take long for your baby to outgrow it. Some people find the rocking facility very useful, but it's worth resisting the temptation to rock your baby to sleep every night or you may be leading to problems in the future.

Whichever you opt for, it's important to buy a new mattress which fits the crib or carrycot properly. Read the crib manufacturer's recommendations before you buy your mattress – they are there for reasons of safety.

Once a baby graduates from this first stage of bed (at anything up to six months old), then most parents choose a standard cot to last for the next couple of years. A cot bed is another option. This is basically a larger than average cot with sides that can be removed when your baby is old enough. Although the use of a cot bed does put off the need to buy a proper bed for your child for some years, if you are planning to have any more children, you'll probably want to have the

I like to rock my baby to sleep in his crib, but my partner says that I'm creating a rod for my own back, as he'll only come to expect it later on.

Beth, mother to Joe, three weeks old.

Babies like to be rocked as it reminds them of the movements they felt when they were in the womb. Having said that, your partner has also got a point, but it's not too late for you to prevent problems occurring. Babies have to learn to go to sleep by themselves, without any help from you, or they will come to expect to get the same help if they wake up in the middle of the night or at some God-forsaken hour of the morning. Ideally, you should put your baby down to sleep when he is sleepy but not actually asleep (after a feed for example) and then leave him to get on with it himself.

Letting him fall asleep in your arms first or rocking him in his cradle may lead to problems if you continue to do it for a matter of months, but a bit of rocking and cradling in the first few weeks may help your baby to feel loved and secure without having any disastrous sleeping habits in the future.

cot free for them in a couple of years anyway. In this case the extra cost of a cot bed may not be worth while.

When it comes to choosing a mattress for the cot, you'll find a bewildering selection of designs and huge differences in their respective prices. Again it's important to get one that fits the cot properly. Then there is a choice of different mattress fillings, from standard foam to much more complex combinations of fibres. In the past there have been cot death scares linked to mattresses filled with certain fire-retardant materials, but these have been shown to be unfounded as yet.

HOW TO POSITION YOUR BABY

Always put your baby down to sleep on his back, with his feet close to the bottom of the crib. This is so that however much he wriggles during the night, he cannot go down the crib any further and end up completely covered by his blankets. As your baby gets older and more mobile he may start turning over in his sleep until he's lying on his tummy, but this is not usually until he is about five or six months or more and past the time when he is most at risk from cot death. If it makes you feel better you could turn him on to his back before you go to bed yourself, but you can guarantee that it won't be long before he's gone back to his favourite position, so there's little point in sitting up all night worrying about it.

WHAT TO DRESS HIM IN FOR BED

This really depends on the season, how warm your house is (and will stay all night) and your baby. If your baby seems to sleep in one tidy position all night with the covers up neatly under his chin, that's fine, but some babies don't keep their covers on for more than a minute, so they will need to go to bed wearing a bit more. While you are gathering confidence and getting to know your new baby, dress him in a layer more than you would need in bed (assuming that you sleep under the same number of sheets and blankets as your baby), then check his body temperature while he sleeps by placing your fingers on the back of his neck and feeling whether he is too hot or cold. If your baby never stays under the bedclothes, then you will have to compensate by adding an extra layer of clothing.

A baby can't control his body temperature in the same way an adult can, so it's up to you to make sure that he doesn't get too hot, which is just as crucial as stopping him from becoming too cold. A recent study into cot death recommends that the bedroom should be at a temperature overnight which is comfortable for a lightly clothed adult (about 16–20°C/60–68°F).

HOW MANY BLANKETS TO USE

This is inextricably linked to the amount of clothes he wears and the other factors mentioned above. Some childcare experts suggest that you think in terms of togs (a measurement indicating the weight and warmth of your bedclothes) and make sure that your baby's bedclothes don't exceed the recommended tog rating for summer and winter. This can all get rather complicated – and I know of one new mother who, as a result, ended up not counting sheep when she went to sleep, but togs, and then dreamt of different numbers and sums all night. The simple solution is that if you feel hot in the room, then keep your baby's bedclothes light; if you feel cold, then give your baby an extra layer of bedclothes too. Having several light layers of blankets keeps a baby warm and comfy and allows you to take off a layer or add one if necessary. It's important that your baby doesn't get too hot so don't use a duvet until he is one year old (they get too hot), and don't pile on the bedclothes if he's feverish or ill (even if that's what your mother did for you when you were a child!). Also don't put him to bed in a hat as he needs to be able to lose heat from his head.

In the early days (up until four weeks) you may find that your baby likes to be swaddled tightly to keep him feeling as confined and secure as he was in your womb. There's no great art to this, just place him down diagonally on a sheet or blanket, then wrap one half over his tummy and under his back. Lift the bottom corner and bring it up over your baby's body, then take the other half of the blanket over his tummy in the opposite direction to the first and under his back once more. Swaddling tightly like this has been known to calm many crying babies too.

DUMMIES AND OTHER AIDS TO SLEEP

Dummies still provoke a lot of debate among parents and childcare professionals, but the bottom line is that if a dummy helps you to settle a fractious baby then it has to be a good thing – for the first few months anyway. It is true that you may find yourself in and out of your baby's room to stick a dummy back in at night, but if that is all you have to do to settle your baby then it's not too much of a hardship. What isn't true is that it will do your baby's mouth any serious damage, as long as he stops using it before his permanent teeth appear. In fact, if you have a sucky baby, dentists agree that it is preferable that he sucks a dummy rather than a thumb. You can't get rid of a thumb when you choose and also it can do more lasting damage to the positioning of the teeth.

Don't worry that if you start using a dummy now, it will become a permanent fixture. You are in control of how much it is used by your baby so it's up to you to set your own limits. Many parents find that a dummy is helpful for the first five months, then their baby either rejects it or the parents take advantage of his lessening interest and dispose of it themselves. Other parents say that they allowed their baby to have it

I encouraged Zachary to adopt a muslin square as a comforter, but I washed and changed in frequently so that he never became attached to one particular one and it wasn't a disaster if we lost it and had to replace it.

Claire, mother to Zachary, nine months old.

for as long as two or three years then chucked it in the bin. Be ready for a few disturbed nights afterwards though.

If you do decide to use one, try to limit its use to in the cot, and for the odd times when your baby is very upset. That way you won't come to rely on it to keep your baby quiet when you'd rather not have to tend to him or hear him cry.

If you are breastfeeding your baby, wait until you think feeding is properly established, usually at around six weeks, before introducing a dummy, as it may cause some nipple confusion. Also make sure that your baby is still feeding at the same rate once he starts to use a dummy, as in some cases a baby gets his sucking satisfaction from that, and doesn't feed as much as he should.

Sometimes a baby just will not take a dummy and will spit it out however often you attempt to persuade him. If this is the case, or you would rather your baby didn't have one anyway, you may want to encourage another comfort object instead – not only for night times, but for the times when your child is feeling insecure or is upset. A baby often adopts his own comforter at around six months old, but you can encourage this by always offering him the same teddy or muslin square at bedtime and by taking it with you whenever you go out.

I put a baby listening monitor in Ailidh's room and kept the parents' unit close by me, especially in the evenings. I could hear her if she cried even without the monitor, but with the volume turned up high I could even hear her breathing which was reassuring. As the months went by I found I was turning the volume down more and more as I became more relaxed!

Katrina, mother to Ailidh, one year old.

Q

The shops are full of bumpers and cot duvets, but a friend of mine told me I shouldn't use them. Why?

Paula, 32 weeks pregnant.

Cot bumpers are pretty and make a cot look more cosy, which is why many new parents succumb to them, but they should be avoided for two important reasons. First, they are tied to the bars of the cot with ribbon which could become tangled around your baby and restrict his movement or, worse, his circulation. Secondly, and more importantly, it is easy for a wriggly baby to become pressed up against the bumper or even get his head underneath it if the bumper comes away from the sides, and that, combined with the risk of overheating significantly increases risk of cot death.

I have become really worried about cot death. So much so that I don't want my baby to move into his own room and I am constantly checking that he is still alive as he sleeps. How much of a risk is it really?

Claire, mother to Isaac, six months old.

It is natural that you will be concerned about your baby and the risk of cot death, and it is wise to check him from time to time once you've put him down to sleep, but try not to let it become an obsession. By the time your baby reaches six months old he is beyond the high-risk stage. There are certain things you can do to reduce the risk even further during the first few months of life: breastfeed your baby; don't smoke or allow others to smoke in the vicinity of your baby and his cot; do not put him down to sleep in your own bed; keep his bedclothes and bedding appropriate to the temperature of the room – don't allow him to overheat or get too cold; always put him down on his back with his feet at the foot of the cot; always seek medical advice promptly if your baby is unwell – especially if he has a raised temperature, breathing difficulties or is less responsive than normal.

I bought lots of sheets for the cot and I'm glad I did. Lucy turned out to be quite a sicky baby and some nights we ended up getting through about four sheets! Sometimes I'd just put another sheet folded under her head, or a muslin square, so that if she was sick we could just take that away without having to completely remake the bed.

Rebecca, mother to Lucy, 18 months old.

PATTERNS OF SLEEP

Over the first six months, your baby's patterns of sleeping will be
continuously changing until eventually, believe it or not, you will realize
that you are actually in some sort of routine – albeit with some hiccups.

THE EARLY DAYS AND WEEKS

In the first few days your baby will sleep for misleadingly long
stretches, lulling many new parents into thinking that this baby
business is a doddle and what on earth have their friends been
complaining about. However, this honeymoon period is only Nature's
way of letting your baby recover after the exhausting process of being
born – and a chance for you to get some much earned rest too. Don't
waste a minute of this time gazing in wonder at what you've created,
make sure that you do get some sleep too – you'll soon be needing it.

A golden rule to remember at this stage is 'never wake a sleeping
baby'. As long as your baby is fit and healthy he will wake up when he
is hungry and it doesn't matter if he sleeps through what you
consider to be a feed time. He'll certainly catch up later on. (Note,
however, that for a baby less than six weeks old to sleep for more
than eight hours at a time is unusual. If this happens you should
check with your doctor.)

By the second week your baby will be getting into the swing of
sleeping and feeding, and doing a lot of the latter, though maybe not
so much of the former. All babies are different and, like us adults,
require differing amounts of sleep – although Murphy's Law
guarantees that you will have the baby who takes only 40 minute
naps, while your friends breed the little angels who would sleep
through an earthquake. On average for the first month of life, a baby
sleeps 16 hours or so a day, but of course that means there are plenty
who sleep for 11 (or less) or 20 (or even more). In between sleeping

your new baby will be doing little more than feeding and having a short wakeful time, but as time goes by you'll notice that the wakeful periods are getting longer and your baby needs a bit more entertaining. Don't worry too much at this stage about putting your baby down at certain times for a sleep or expect to have a routine, just

Q

My baby is still confusing night and day it seems. She wakes up all the time at night and sleeps much more solidly during the day. What can I do?

Mandy, mother to Ruth, five weeks old.

In the womb, babies often seem to come to life at night so it's not surprising that many still like to do that once they have been born. If you are breastfeeding your baby, she will still need to be fed once or twice at night at five weeks old so you can't expect her to sleep through yet, but you can encourage her to take more of her feeds in the day time and sleep for longer at night if you can teach her the difference between night and day. For some babies this comes easily but with others you can help by keeping the cot as a place for night time only and putting her down to sleep elsewhere, such as her pram or a reclining chair, during the day. Also invest in some blackout curtains or a blind for her bedroom so that she associates the dark with night time and sleeping.

If, at five or six months, your baby is still waking at night wanting to be fed, you can be sure that she is not really hungry, just after a bit of comfort, and you may need to do a bit of firmer sleep training (see page 59).

be led by your baby – he's probably got more idea of what he needs than you, at the moment!

TWO TO SIX MONTHS

By 8 to 12 weeks you may notice that your baby is conking out at a similar time each night and his sleeps are becoming a bit more predictable. He may be sleeping about 15 hours a day and a pattern may be emerging of waking at a similar time each morning, having a feed then a short wakeful time, then another nap before a lunchtime feed, then another nap and feed before a more wakeful period in the early evening. If you're lucky he may even be sleeping from the time he has a last feed at night (when you go to bed, say) until 5 or 6 in the morning as by this time he should be able to sleep for six hours at night. Of course some babies may be wakeful all day and sleep longer at night – there are no rules.

You can help this pattern to develop and suit your lifestyle by adding some constants, such as a regular bath and bedtime, and entertaining him to stretch the time between feeds. Encourage him to sleep more at the times when you want sleep (normally between 11 pm and 6 am!) by perhaps waking him for a feed before you go to bed. If you need to go to bed earlier then perhaps you could express some milk or offer a formula feed for your partner to give him while you rest.

By 16 weeks your baby should be sleeping twice as long at night as during the day, with about eight or ten hours of sleep being the average at night, between 7 pm and 7 am.

OVER SIX MONTHS

By six or seven months your baby will be on solid food and hopefully into a more regular routine of feeding and sleeping. About three-quarters of babies are now sleeping through the night, and the day may go something like this:

6.30 am	Wake – milk
7.30 am	Breakfast and drink
	Sleep
	Mid-morning – milk
12.30 pm	Lunch and drink
	Sleep
	Mid-afternoon milk
5 pm	Tea and drink
7.30 pm	Milk
	Bed

By one year babies usually need about 13–14 hours of sleep a day. They still need two daytime naps, but the shorter mid-morning nap will be needed less and less.

My baby was always a very restless sleeper at night, until someone told me how noisy it was in the womb and I began to wonder if it might actually be too quiet in our room at night time! I brought a ticking alarm clock into our room and put it near the cot, in the hope that it might soothe him. It may be a coincidence, but it seemed to do the trick!

Sally, mother to Ben, five months old.

Q

At the moment my baby goes to bed at 9 pm, but I want to bring forward her bedtime, so that I can sit and have a quiet dinner with my husband at a reasonable hour. How can I do it? I don't want her to wake up any earlier.

Marie-Claude, mother to Morgane, six months old.

If you have already established a good bedtime routine (see page 54) then it will be easier to bring forwards the actual time you put her down to sleep, as she will recognize all the cues that bedtime is on its way. Assuming that you have a routine, all you need to do then is gradually bring the time forward – say by half an hour every few days. By six months it is reasonable to expect your baby to go down at 7.30 pm (some settle even earlier) so it should only take three steps before you achieve your goal. Be prepared for a couple of early wakings while she gets used to the idea – and for the amount of sleep she takes during the day to be reduced.

 A

I found that when I had my baby in the bedroom with me at night I would always pick him up if he made the slightest whimper and I'm sure we disturbed one another with our movements. I'd always planned to keep my baby in the same room as me for the first few months, but in the end we discovered that we all got a better night's sleep if he was in a room of his own.

Amanda, mother to Michael, one year old.

I think it's crucial to have a routine – it's the only way to survive. I also do as much as possible in the way of chores in the evenings when the girls are asleep as it's virtually impossible to do anything when they are awake.

Jackie, mother to Holly and Chloe, 18 months old.

TWINS AND SLEEP

If, as a mother of newborn twins, you have a low expectation of the amount of sleep you are going to get for the first few months, then you will not be disappointed!

The first few weeks are bound to be a bit shaky, but it will improve. Feeding your babies together will help as they are then likely to go to sleep at the same time and this will avoid you being up all night feeding one and then the other. Many parents find it helps in the early days if they wake the second baby when the first wakes for a feed. After a few weeks of doing this they begin to wake, feed and sleep in unison – if you are lucky! Don't worry too much about one waking the other at other times though, it's more than likely that they will be able to sleep through whatever noise the other can make, even if you can't. If one does turn out to be a worse sleeper than the other though, then you will have to consider putting them in separate rooms while you try the sleep training routine (see page 59).

It is important that you sleep whenever you get the chance. Do not worry at this stage about having 'quality' time with them as individuals and attempting to play with one while the other sleeps – you will be a better mother if you feel a bit more rested.

GETTING A ROUTINE GOING

Bedtime routines are very useful things. Babies like and respond to familiar rituals as they help to make them feel secure and comforted – which of course are just the sort of feelings you want to instil at bedtime. A routine can help a baby wind down gradually and let him know that bedtime is on the way so that by the time you put him down he is more than ready to drift happily off to sleep. Another real bonus is that it will help you to settle him on those occasions when everything else is rather different or strange, such as at Christmas time or when you stay away from home.

It is best to start a routine as soon as you can, but that doesn't mean the day you bring him home from hospital. Those first few weeks are so tiring and unpredictable that establishing any sort of routine is virtually impossible – and when a baby is feeding every three hours who is to say when his bedtime actually is?

The best time to start is when you feel that life is getting a bit more settled and predictable – perhaps at around two to three months old. You may find that a routine naturally evolves, but if things get a bit hectic and haphazard in your home after 6 pm, try to start bringing in some constants that your baby will recognize as a cue that bedtime is nigh. A common routine may go as follows:

6.30 pm bathtime   A tired, grumpy baby will often perk up and enjoy splashing in the bath with some toys. Don't worry that it will wake him up too much so that he will not go to sleep, a bath usually helps to relax a baby too.

6.50 pm pyjama time   Some quiet play and fun are fine, but forget real high frolics that will wind him up again.

7 pm milktime   When your baby gets older you could add storytime at this stage too.

7.30 pm bedtime   Put him down, give him a goodnight kiss and
   perhaps a comforter, such as blanket, teddy or dummy. Switch on
   the musical mobile if he likes that, then leave.

The key is to keep routines simple. Start kissing every teddy bear in
your child's room goodnight or performing other such antics and you'll
soon find that it's taking two hours to put your baby to bed. It needs to
be a routine that you will follow every day, however tired you are; your
baby will soon come to expect it and feel disorientated if you drop the
routine one week and pick it up the next.

*We're going on holiday next week, how can I keep our
routine going then?*

Anna, mother to Emma, eight months old.

Bedtime routines are very useful when you are on
holiday as they will help your baby feel secure – even
though she's far from home. It doesn't matter that you're
not in the same bathroom or the same bed, still try to go
through the motions of bath (even if it's in a shower or
washing-up bowl!), milk, bed – and don't forget your
baby's comfort objects whatever you do! You may find
your baby isn't as easy to lull to sleep as usual, but at
least you will have made her feel as reassured as possible.

With twins, I need to be really organized, so I start winding them
down at about 5.30 pm each evening with a gentle massage before
their bath. They love it and it really relaxes them for bed.

Helen, mother to Kim and Victoria, five months old.

Q

The time at which my partner comes in each night varies, but it's usually at about the time Nathan goes to sleep. He obviously wants to play with Nathan just at the time I want to put him to bed and don't want him wound up. What do you suggest?

Claire, mother to Nathan, ten months old.

You're right – it's best not to let your baby get involved in fatherly rough and tumbles just before bedtime as it will make it harder for you to settle him afterwards, but your partner could enjoy some special time with your baby by taking over the bedtime routine instead of you – that way you also get a chance to put your feet up too! When he comes in, why not get your partner to share a bath with your baby or read him a story while he has his milk? It will help in the long-term too, if your baby does not come to expect you to be the sole settler at bedtime.

We started a routine when James was about six months and find it really helps now if he gets overtired and needs an early night. We just start the bedtime routine much earlier and by the time he's gone through his milk, story and kiss he is more than happy for us to turn out the light.

Kate, mother to James, one year old.

SLEEP PROBLEMS

Sleep deprivation is horrendous –
a real form of torture. And while
most of us are happy to suffer it
for the first few months of our
babies' lives in recognition that
they still need frequent feeds, if
you are still not getting enough
sleep six months later, it can be
hard to cope with. In the early
weeks, a baby usually wakes
because he's hungry, but by the
time he's reached four months
old he shouldn't need any extra
calories at night and all he's after

is the comfort of a regularly filled tummy – or cuddles from you. If you
are still being woken at night, first try the following (one at a time), in
this order:

✿ Check that he's getting enough to eat during the day. It may be that he
   needs to catch up on his feeds at night time. If you are breastfeeding
   try nursing a bit more frequently. If you are bottlefeeding try giving
   him an extra few millilitres at each feed.

✿ Increase the amount you give him at bedtime. Tickle his toes or nudge
   him if he seems to be falling asleep before he's had an adequate
   amount.

✿ Wake your baby up for a feed before you go to sleep. You may find
   he's too sleepy to feed properly, but it may give him enough
   sustenance to keep him quiet while you have six hours or so of sleep.

✿ Don't jump to feed him at the slightest whimper. Perhaps try putting
   him in his own room, or educate yourself to wait for a while before you
   pick him up – you never know, he may settle back to sleep by himself.

- If you do pick him up, try giving him a cuddle or rocking him to calm him, but don't feed him. He may just want a bit of comfort from you.
- If he takes a cup or bottle, offer him just water not milk – he may decide that it's not worth waking up for just a bit of H_2O.
- If, after trying all of the above, you have to offer him milk to calm him, then try to cut back on the amount you offer – either by a few minutes, if you are breastfeeding, or by diluting the formula, if he has a bottle. Keep decreasing the amount gradually until he just decides not to bother.

Q

When I finally get my baby to sleep it seems to be in my arms after a feed, in the sling, or over my shoulder after a lot of pacing up and down. Then, as soon as I put her down in her cot, she wakes up again. Is there anything I can do?

Emma, mother to Rose, five weeks old.

In the next few weeks you need to work towards putting your baby into the cot before she has dropped off completely so that she learns to go to sleep in there, not on you. In the meantime, try to prepare the sleeping area before you get into the motions of feeding and rocking so that the blankets are pulled back and the light is already low. Ideally feed or rock her in the room in which she sleeps. Notice which side you find it easiest to hold your baby when you put her down into the cot, then try to feed or carry her on that side last of all. When you reach the crib, keep your baby as close to you for as long as possible as you lower her in so that she feels warm and secure, then keep your hands on her for a few seconds after you have put her down.

SLEEP TRAINING

If at six months your baby is still waking at night on a regular basis, it could be time to get firm. You don't want to upset your baby, but equally, you can't allow him to disturb the whole family at night. What's needed is a gentle, but firm approach – one that lets your baby know that you are in control, but also never allows him to become fearful or be left crying hysterically. The trick is to let your baby know that you will come and see him if he needs you, but that as all he'll get is some gentle calming, it probably isn't worth waking up for!

Consultant paediatrician Dr Christopher Green has been an advocate of this 'controlled crying technique' since 1974 and claims to have had considerable success with babies as young as six months. Here's the plan: First, don't run to your baby the instant he cries out, wait for a couple of minutes then go and comfort him, but ideally without picking him out of the cot. When the crying has subsided return to your bed. If he starts to cry again, leave him for a bit longer than the first time before you go in and just repeat the soothing process. Don't hang around rocking him back to a deep sleep or feeding him – he'll only come to expect it. As soon as he's calm, head back to your own bed.

This may go on for some time, but each time leave him for a little bit longer before you go in to see him – and eventually he'll get the picture.

The key to this working though is determination and firmness on your part. If you start this you have to see it through – however long it takes each night, and for however many nights it takes. Dr Green has found an 80 per cent cure within one to three weeks, most within the first week – so there is light at the end of the tunnel. Don't choose a time when anyone in the family is ill or has got an important meeting looming though – you have to be feeling strong!

I used to rush into Matilda at the slightest noise, but she seemed to be forever waking up. Then a friend suggested that I leave her a few minutes – and, unbelievably, she went back to sleep herself. Now I realize that she often makes a few jerky movements and calls out in her sleep, without waking up at all. I must previously have been waking her up myself with all my efforts to soothe her!

Beccy, mother to Matilda, six months old.

My baby is blind, so I do not know how to help him distinguish night from day and sleep for longer at night time.

Mo, mother to Jack, two weeks old.

It can take a blind or partially sighted baby longer to develop this skill, but you can give him plenty of help. A routine is going to be even more important for you and your baby, for all aspects of life, and it will be especially helpful as a method of giving your baby clues that night time and bedtime are on the way. As soon as you feel able, establish a regular bath and bedtime, and try to add other clues, such as singing him a lullaby, when you put him down to sleep. In most areas there are sleep clinics especially for children with special needs, so if you continue to have sleep problems, get in touch with them via your health visitor or doctor.

Q

My baby was in the special care baby unit for a couple of weeks before she came home. She is fine now, but it is hard to get her to sleep at night still, although she sleeps well in the daytime.

Liz, mother to Amy, three weeks old.

You may find that the reason is that it is too dark and quiet in your baby's room at night. In the special care baby unit there is a constant buzz of noise all day and night, and the lights, although sometimes dimmed at night, are never off completely. Try playing a radio at a low volume in her room and keeping a nightlight on – it may help to recreate the situation she is used to and help her to feel more secure so that she will drop off to sleep more easily.

I encouraged Josie to become attached to her muslin square as a comforter and now it really helps her to go back to sleep if she's upset. Apparently babies become attached to certain things at around six months if you allow them. Muslin squares are great because they are easily replaceable and can be washed too!

Lucy, mother to Josie, nine months old.

Survival tips

Do not expect your baby to sleep through the night for the first six months. Who knows – you might then be pleasantly surprised.

✿

A baby can sleep in most places and be comfortable – it is only your friends who might be impressed by a fancy crib.

✿

Always put your baby down on his back with his feet at the bottom of the crib.

✿

Overheating his room is dangerous. Keep it at a temperature you find comfortable when you are dressed in your nightclothes.

✿

Start a routine of bath, milk, bed as soon as you feel able. It will help to prepare your baby for a good, long (we hope) sleep.

✿

Don't let your baby's bad sleeping habits upset the whole family. Adopt a gentle, but firm approach if the night wakings or settling times get out of hand.

3

Feeding your baby

BREAST OR BOTTLE?

For the first four months of her life, all your baby needs to thrive is milk, provided either directly from you or from a bottle. Whether or not you decide to breastfeed your baby is obviously a personal decision, but if you are still undecided about which path to take, you might consider the following points.

REASONS FOR BREASTFEEDING

❀ No formula milk can reproduce Nature's recipe. Your breastmilk will adapt and change as your baby's requirements alter. Its composition is different in the morning to the afternoon, more watery when it is hot in the summer and it subtly changes as your baby gets older too.

❀ Formula milk is an artificial substance, made from modified cow's milk, and feeding it to your baby before her immune system has had a chance to develop any resistance of its own can result in a higher incidence of gastroenteritis. It may also sensitize her to potential allergens, making her more likely to develop allergies, such as eczema or asthma – especially if you have a family history of such problems.

✿ Colostrum, the initial 'milk' the baby obtains from your breast in the first few days, acts as a barrier to invading bacteria and provides your baby with antibodies to the diseases to which you are resistant – vital protection in those vulnerable early days. It is also a concentrated, protein-rich substance, satisfying all your baby's early nutritional requirements.

✿ Breastfeeding helps to create an immediate bond between you and your baby – especially if you put your baby to the breast soon after the birth and enjoy the skin-to-skin contact it brings.

✿ Feeding sessions make you sit down and rest, which you need in the early weeks. Breastfeeding usually takes a little longer than bottlefeeding and can't be handed over to someone else – so you benefit from the time spent with your feet up while your baby enjoys her feed.

✿ As you breastfeed your baby in the early days, the oxytocin hormone you produce helps your uterus to contract and return to its normal size more quickly.

✿ Creating breastmilk burns plenty of calories (up to 600 a day) so, although you may eat more than ever before while you are feeding your baby, most mothers who breastfeed find that they get back into shape more quickly.

My mother-in-law constantly maintained that my baby would be better off on the bottle – mostly, I suspect, because she wanted to feed her herself. I was really glad that I stuck to my guns and persevered with breastfeeding. It was a decision I was happy with and I was sure I was doing the best for my Hannah.

Karen, mother to Hannah, six months old.

❀ Breastfeeding is better for your baby's bottom! Breastfed babies are less prone to stomach upsets and diarrhoea, their bowel movements smell somewhat sweeter than those of formula-fed babies and they are less likely to have nappy rash.

❀ It's always on tap! There's always a meal up your jumper if you get delayed or your baby unexpectedly needs a drink. You also don't have to get up in the night to warm a bottle and there's no sterilizing of bottles to worry about.

❀ Breastmilk is free. You'll have to buy some nursing bras, and a supply of breast pads, but that's it.

REASONS FOR BOTTLEFEEDING

❀ If you want to share the feeding with your partner or another carer, bottlefeeding will allow you to hand the baby over whenever you are tired or need to go out. However, even if you are breast-feeding you could also express some milk into a bottle for the times your partner wants to feed the baby – or you could add one or two formula feeds to your day (see Combining breast and bottle, page 84).

❀ Personal choice. You may simply not like the idea of breastfeeding. If you've heard stories about how people have tried to feed their babies themselves and given up, you may have decided you can't face the hassle. Or you may not fancy the idea of being tied to your baby so completely for so many months (see Combining breast and bottle, page 84).

❀ You would feel awkward about breastfeeding in public. Thankfully these days most people hardly bat an eyelid at breastfeeding mums, and there are a lot more public facilities for mothers, but some people still find the idea embarrassing. If you do, try sticking a teddy bear under your jumper as if he were feeding and take a look

at yourself in the mirror – you see it can be done quite discreetly!
There are also shirts and jumpers now available which allow you to
open a 'pocket' over your breast and feed your baby through that –
so you need not reveal an inch of flesh!

✿ You can eat and drink what you like. True, you don't have to worry
about last night's bottle of Chianti being passed straight through to
your baby – but you still have to cope with the hangover!

✿ You know how much your baby is having to drink. Yes, Nature really
let us down when she didn't give us see-through breasts to let us
monitor our babies' feeds. Babies do tend to take only what they
need, but it is more reassuring when you can measure that in
millilitres or fluid ounces.

If you are still unsure which way to go, try not to think of it in black
and white terms – there is plenty of room for flexibility, so don't feel
you have to be totally committed one way or the other for ever. You
could just have a go at breastfeeding to see how you get on, then
perhaps move onto a combination of breast and bottle if that suits you
better. It is best to give breastfeeding a fair trial though and commit
yourself to it for at least six weeks before you decide whether or not to
introduce the odd bottle or switch to bottlefeeding completely. Six
weeks allows time for the feeding to get well established, and
introducing a teat before then can confuse your baby and prevent her
from settling at the breast properly.

Whether you breastfeed or bottlefeed eventually, it is essential that
you are happy with the decision you make. What may be best for your
baby's nutrition may still not be the right choice to make if it leaves you
feeling anxious and unhappy in the early weeks with your baby. A
happy mother makes for a happy baby, so don't feel pressurized by
anyone into making a particular decision – it really is up to you.

BREASTFEEDING – THE BASICS

WHAT YOU'LL NEED

Nature has already supplied you with the most vital equipment for breastfeeding – so you don't have to go out and invest in sterilizing equipment and formula milk. Don't worry if your breasts are small – the size of your breasts has no relation to the amount of milk you can produce, and babies can often latch on more easily to a smaller breast. The beauty of breastmilk is that there is always enough for your baby at the right temperature and perfectly sterile. You don't even have to wash your breasts before you feed your baby, as she'll probably prefer to feed from a breast that smells of you, rather than a fancy soap.

You'll find the following useful:

Three feeding bras   These are
different from normal bras in
that they allow you to release
each cup quickly and easily
to feed your baby. Some
have zips running under
each breast while others
have small release
clasps on the straps.
Even if you don't
normally wear a
bra, you should
invest in these.
Your breasts will
be at least one
cup size larger
than normal
once your milk

comes in a few days after the birth and they will need plenty of support to keep them in shape. A feeding bra will also allow you to hold the breast pads in place (see below). It is vital that you are fitted for a feeding bra by a professional in the last few weeks of the pregnancy or once your milk comes in so that it fits you properly. A bra that is too tight will not only be uncomfortable, it could lead to a painful blocked milk duct and mastitis (an inflammation of the breast tissue).

Breast pads   You can buy washable or disposable breast pads. The washable ones inevitably work out to be quite a bit cheaper in the end as you can get through hundreds of pads when you are feeding. You are also likely to have the washing machine on all the time anyway once the baby has been born! With disposable pads, you do seem to get what you pay for – the cheaper ones being less well shaped or less absorbent.

Nipple cream   Many new mums never need to touch this stuff and sail through feeding without a thought to their nipples, but if you don't buy some before you start feeding, you can guarantee that you'll be the one who develops problems in the first few days. Creams containing calendula or camomile are great for soothing

I had such leaky breasts that I used to soak a breast pad every time I breastfed. I decided I should collect the milk rather than wasting it all. I bought some special breastshields and wore one while I fed Harry on the other breast. I collected so much milk in the shield each time that it didn't take long to fill a bottle for another feed!

Denise, mother to Harry, four years old.

sore nipples and helping them to heal – and if you don't use it for your nipples it is also a wonderful treatment for your baby if she has dry skin or nappy rash!

Breast pump   This is only a necessity if you decide to express some milk from your breasts to feed your baby from a bottle. Before you buy one it may be worth borrowing one from a friend to see how you get on with it. Some women find expressing a doddle, while others think it the most degrading and awkward experience in the world! You can choose from manual or battery-operated pumps – or you may find that you can successfully express by just squeezing the area around your areola (the brown area around your nipple) yourself. Obviously, if you do decide to express milk, you will also need to invest in the bottlefeeding paraphernalia listed on page 78 to ensure that everything is sterile.

If you are worried that you are not producing enough milk, never introduce a bottle as a top-up. That is the beginning of the end as far as breastfeeding is concerned. The best way of increasing your milk supply is to feed your baby more often, as the more your baby seems to want, the more milk you will produce. Put your baby to the breast frequently (even if she doesn't seem to want it) for a couple of days or, ideally go to bed with your baby for a day and let her feed on and off all day, while you are resting too. Breastfeeding works on the principle of supply and demand.

Corinne, midwife.

HOW TO BREASTFEED YOUR BABY

Strange as it may seem, what should be the most natural thing in the world does take a bit of learning – for you and your baby. You should be given plenty of help and support in establishing breastfeeding by your midwives – and don't be afraid to ask for it if it is not forthcoming.

✿ First, get yourself comfortable. Sit with your back well supported and surrounded by cushions. You need to bring your baby to your breast, not your breast down to your baby, so it may help to use a cushion to support your baby and your arms, particularly the arm supporting her head. Make sure that you are relaxed and have no tension in your neck and shoulders.

✿ Encourage your baby to turn to the breast by stroking the cheek nearest you until she turns to the nipple. It won't take long for your baby to associate your breasts with feeding, but for the first few days you may need to encourage her to look in the right direction.

- ✿ Make sure she is 'latched on' properly. It's important to check that your baby has got her mouth around your nipple correctly. The action of breastfeeding is completely different to that of sucking from a bottle. In fact, it requires a 'chomping' rather than a sucking action – your baby's jaw needs to be moving up and down, and her mouth needs to be open wide around the areola, not just the nipple, in order to encourage the milk flow. Take a look at where the jawbone meets your baby's ears – if you can see movement there and her ears are wiggling, the chances are she's latched on well.

- ✿ Don't pull her off the breast half way through a feed. Many babies will release their suck as they fall asleep or have had enough, but if you need to release her yourself, then gently put a finger between her gums to open them slightly. If you just pull her off you will develop very sore nipples.

- ✿ Drain at least one breast completely. Once your baby is feeding well she should be able to take most of the milk she needs in the first five minutes, but many babies make mealtimes a far longer affair than that and will spend even three-quarters of an hour slowly chomping away and enjoying the closeness and comfort that feeding brings. Be guided by your baby not the clock and let her feed until she has emptied one breast completely, then see if she is interested in taking some milk from the other breast too. At the next feed offer the second breast first.

Throw out the clock. The idea of feeding your baby only every four hours is out of date and unnatural. Don't necessarily feed your baby every time she whimpers (she may just want a cuddle), but every time she cries urgently and insistently, she is hungry and needs feeding – even if it is only two hours since the last feed began.

Annette, health visitor.

Q ────────────────────────

My five-week-old baby isn't putting on enough weight according to the centile charts in my baby's health development book, but she seems to be happy enough. My health visitor has suggested that I bottlefeed or give her a bottle as a top-up, but I didn't want to introduce cow's milk for as long as possible because we have a history of allergies in the family.

Tina, mother to Ella, five weeks old.

If your baby is actually losing weight, that is a cause for concern, but if your baby is putting on some weight (however little) is producing plenty of wet and dirty nappies and seems happy, then there should not be any cause to worry. Centile charts are a guide to the expected weight gain for an average baby, so it is better to look at the baby as a whole rather than just a chart. Consider how she is looking, whether she is feeding regularly enough and so on. Only if her weight drops two centile lines might it be a cause for concern.

It is frustrating sometimes that we cannot tell how much a breastfed baby is getting, but if you can feel your breasts tingling as the milk is 'let down' when your baby starts to feed then you can be sure there is nothing wrong with your milk supply. If you are keen to continue breastfeeding, then it is best not to offer your baby a bottle, but instead concentrate on getting breastfeeding well established. First, make sure that she is well latched onto the breast. Ask a midwife, health visitor or breastfeeding counsellor to check as you feed your baby. Secondly you need to build up your milk supply. Make sure you are eating a good diet, drinking plenty of fluids and resting well. Then, for a few days, try feeding your baby more often – even if she doesn't ask for it. Allow your baby to completely empty one breast when she feeds and nurse for as long as she likes on the second too. Don't let her drop off to sleep until you are sure that she has had enough to eat. After a few days you should notice that your breasts appear fuller and you have more milk. Milk production is a matter of supply and demand – the more your baby drinks, the more you will produce.

My baby doesn't seem to like feeding from one side as much as the other. I didn't mind too much at first, but now one of my breasts is significantly larger than the other.

Elizabeth, mother to Joanna, six weeks old.

Babies often have a preference for feeding one side – perhaps because we are more adept at holding them one side than the other or simply because they like to lie on one side more than the other. You could try to stimulate the milk supply on the less favoured side by expressing from it when your baby feeds from the other breast, but this may not stimulate your baby's interest in it. Don't worry unduly as the breasts will even out after you wean your baby from the breast.

SOME COMMON CONCERNS

Some women sail through breastfeeding while others find it a bit of a struggle at first. The key to preventing it from being a painful experience is to get your baby properly positioned on the breast. Point the nipple to the roof of the baby's mouth, ensuring that she has a good mouthful of areola, particularly the lower portion. She is not supposed to be latched onto the nipple itself. Ask your midwife, health visitor or breastfeeding counsellor to check the way you are holding her too. She should be lying on her side, so you are tummy to tummy with her head slightly higher than her body. Make sure you are bringing her to your breast not dropping your breast to down her.

If your nipples are still sore after your baby has adopted a good position, look after them by using nipple cream, avoiding soap on them and exposing them to air as much as possible. You should continue feeding from them, but try starting feeds on the less sore nipple so that it doesn't have to endure the most vigorous sucking. If your nipples are equally sore, alternate the breast you start with at each feed or try protective nipple shields. You could also try feeding her in a lying down position so that she is putting pressure on a different part of the nipple.

If your breasts are sore and feel overfull they may be engorged. This commonly happens when the milk first comes in and only lasts a day or two, but it can recur if your baby misses a feed or doesn't empty your breasts properly. Sometimes they are so full your baby can't latch on properly (especially if your breasts are large), in which case you could express off a little milk by hand. Warmth can help to ease the discomfort, so try covering them with warm towels or bathing them with warm water.

Occasionally, mothers develop an infection of the breast called mastitis. The symptoms usually include a shiny, red, tender patch on the breast, and feverish flu-like feelings. If you think you might be suffering from this, see your doctor as soon as you can. It'll clear up quickly with antibiotics, but may develop into an abscess if not dealt with promptly. You can ease the pain by covering your breast with hot and cold flannels alternately and feeding your baby frequently. (Some people also recommend covering the breast with a wet leaf from a Savoy cabbage!) Get as much rest as you can until you feel better.

If your baby suffers from a lot of wind, her digestive system may be reacting to something in your diet. It's difficult to say what foods will cause this and how long the offending ingredient takes to come through into the milk. I think the main thing to remember is that everything is fine in moderation. There is a lot said about what foods you should avoid while you are breastfeeding in case you upset your baby's digestion (namely spicy foods, broccoli, garlic and so on) but a little of what you fancy every now and then is not going to do her any harm.

The one thing that is for sure is that alcohol gets into the bloodstream (and therefore the baby's milk) immediately so it is best not to allow yourself to reach the wobbly stage when you are breastfeeding. Ideally you should keep to the limits you set yourself when you were pregnant – stick to wine or beer instead of spirits and only have a couple of units a week.

Some breastfeeding mothers, desperate for a wild night out, offer their babies a bottle of either expressed or formula milk while they suspect their breast milk is a bit too alcohol rich, and then express the alcohol-laced milk down the drain. I personally found it easier to abstain while I was breastfeeding – primarily because I could not face the thought of tending to a baby while suffering from a hangover.

*My four-week-old baby is feeding non-stop in the evenings,
although in the day and at night time he seems happy to
feed every three or four hours. What should I do?*

Suzy, mother to Tom, four weeks old.

Go with the flow is the simple answer – although
probably not the one you wanted to hear right now! For
the first six weeks or so, while breastfeeding is being
established, your baby will want to feed frequently –
especially in the evenings as it will help to stimulate
your milk supply for the following day. It may also be
because your milk is thinner at the end of a busy day
and your baby needs to feed more often to be filled up,
or it could be that he enjoys the comfort – you'll never
really know. For now, you'll find it easier to cope with if
you accept that this is what your baby needs and you
can't fight it. Try to stretch out the gaps between feeds
by distracting him if you can, but if not, get a good video
or book, put your feet up and relax. The good news is
that this stage will not last forever. By about 11 or 12
weeks you should notice that your baby is feeding less
frequently and your evenings are becoming your own
once more. However, also look out for the growth spurts
when your baby will suddenly seem to be forever
hungry again. These usually occur at three weeks, six
weeks and three months.

Q

I can put my baby to bed easily at night time, but when he wakes up for the 3 am breastfeed I find it really difficult to settle him again. We end up rocking him to sleep for ages, while he cries, or taking him into bed with us, neither of which I want to get into the habit of doing. What are the alternatives?

Gina, mother to George, three weeks old.

It is often easier to get your baby to settle at the end of the day, as he may have been quite active in the early evening and has tired himself out. As you are breastfeeding you may find you are also feeding him frequently in the evenings which is both tiring and satisfying for your baby, helping him to drift off to sleep more easily. When he wakes in the middle of the night he is hungry and may also be missing your warmth. Make sure that you are satisfying his hunger primarily – often babies fall asleep while they are feeding before they have had enough, so work at keeping him awake and feed him for a bit longer than you have been. If that doesn't work then it may be simply that he wants to be close to you. You could allow him to drop off to sleep next to you then pop him in the cot (though Murphy's Law guarantees that he'll wake up at that point!), try swaddling him tightly when you put him back down or perhaps offer him a dummy. The important thing to realize is that it's early days for both you, your baby and the breastfeeding, and things may soon settle down.

A

BOTTLEFEEDING – THE BASICS

WHAT YOU'LL NEED

Six 250ml (8oz) feeding bottles Although to begin with your baby may only be taking a very small amount of milk, by the time she's six months old she may be having as much as 250ml (8oz) at a time, so it's best to start with the larger bottles.

Six teats Although feeding bottles tend to come with teats supplied, they are usually not the flatter orthodontic shape nor specially designed for newborns. Start instead with a slow-flowing teat designed for a new baby or, if you are switching from breast to bottle, go for a variable-flow teat if possible.

Bottle brush This is an essential tool for cleaning the bottles thoroughly.

A means of sterilization This could be simply sterilizing tablets and a bucket, or you may prefer to go for a more modern alternative such as an electric steam sterilizer or a microwave steam sterilizer.

A measuring jug This is useful if you are making up several bottles at once.

A clean knife You'll need this for levelling off the powdered milk in the scoop.

Formula milk There are a number of varieties on the market, the most common being based on demineralized whey protein, a small amount of skimmed milk and a mixture of animal fats and vegetable oils. However there are also milks for hungry babies (based on casein with added carbohydrate), and vegan babies (not containing any animal products).

A bottle warmer A bit of a luxury item (although useful for night feeds), this electrically controlled device is designed to heat your bottle then switch off, so it doesn't become overheated. Of course you could just use a beaker of hot water.

HOW TO MAKE UP FEEDS

Cleanliness and food safety are essential issues when you are bottlefeeding. Your baby could easily develop a gastrointestinal infection if the equipment is not properly sterilized and the milk not appropriately stored. Everything that comes into contact with your baby's food and mouth should be washed and sterilized before use until your baby is at least six months old even if it's only a bottle filled with water.

✿ Wash all the equipment in hot water and a little detergent and scrub the bottles with the brush. Turn the teats inside out to make sure they are thoroughly clean. Rinse both the bottles and teats under hot running water.

✿ Follow the instructions on your sterilizing equipment and fill the bottles with milk as soon as they have been sterilized – they don't stay sterile if left standing around for a day.

✿ Use freshly boiled water that has been left to cool for a while. Don't use bottled water, water that has been softened by a chemical softener or water that has been filtered through a charcoal filter. Mix up the milk in the bottles according to the manufacturer's instructions – never add more or less formula to the bottle than they suggest as you'll only deprive your baby of either water or nourishment. If you are making up a day's worth of feeds it might be easier to use a measuring jug and do the whole lot in one go.

✿ Once you've made up the feeds, keep them in the fridge until you need them, but only make up 24 hours worth of feeds at once so that they are fresh for your baby. If you need to take a bottle out for the day with you, carry it in an insulated carrier so that it stays cold until you use it. Bacteria breed remarkably quickly in warm conditions so never give your baby a bottle that has been heated up for over an hour, or left on a warm windowsill – and never reheat a feed.

✿ To warm the bottle, stand it in a bowl of warm water and shake it occasionally. Test the temperature by spilling a few drops of milk on the inside of your wrist before you give it to your baby

HOW TO BOTTLEFEED YOUR BABY

Bottlefeeding can be as intimate an experience as breastfeeding your baby, if you allow it.

✿ Get the two of you comfortable and allow plenty of time for a feed so that she does not feel rushed and can enjoy the intimate contact with you. Some women like to take their top off so they can enjoy some skin-to-skin closeness with their baby.

✿ Hold her close to you, with her head supported in the crook of your elbow. She should be in a half sitting rather than a lying position so that she can swallow easily and less wind is trapped.

✿ Stroke the cheek nearest to you to encourage her to turn towards you and the teat, then gently put the teat into her mouth.

✿ When she begins to suck at the teat, tilt the bottle so that the teat stays full of milk all the time you are feeding her. This will reduce the amount of air that she swallows. If she seems to be drinking too quickly, or is getting frustrated at the teat, you may need to switch to a slower or faster style of teat. Experiment until you find one that your baby is happy with, then stick to that.

FEEDING TWINS

It may seem hard to believe, but breastfeeding twins is actually a lot easier to put into practice than bottlefeeding – especially if you don't have someone to share the work with. Although it can take longer to establish and does mean the responsibility of feeds falls more exclusively on the mother's shoulders, it does eliminate the work involved with sterilizing bottles and preparing feeds – and of course combined feeding is always an option if you want to get an early night and hand the babies over to your partner.

Make sure that you are eating a good diet (you'll need an extra 500 calories per baby) and that you rest as much as you can. Breastfeeding can be exhausting – especially when there are two babies demanding to be fed every few hours!

To breastfeed both babies at once you need to find a position that works for you and them. Most common is to rest each baby on a pillow with their feet behind you and heads at the breast, or you could try crossing their bodies in front of you. Make sure that you always offer them a different breast at the start of each feed so that if one baby takes more than the other you don't get lopsided breasts.

It is also possible to bottlefeed one baby while you breastfeed the other if you find that suits you better – ideally alternating between the babies.

If you decide to bottlefeed you can try to do them both at once by propping them up on a pillow, in their car seats or in baby chairs in front of you while you hold the two bottles. It is easier if someone can help you out at first. The drawback with feeding them one at a time is that it takes so much longer and, when you are providing six feeds or more a day, you end up spending your whole day either preparing bottles or feeding.

It's lovely having twins, but sometimes I do think that I've missed out on the closeness that a mother can have with one baby. I can't cuddle my babies while I feed them because I have to feed them together while they sit in their seats, and there are always two to juggle.

Sian, mother to Emily and Esther, 11 months old.

Q

I am breastfeeding my twins, but can't seem to find a position to feed them in which is comfortable and practical. In the nursing home they said to put them both on a pillow on the bed and bend over them, but books on breastfeeding say to never take your breasts to the baby, but bring your baby to the breast. Have you got any suggestions?

Cary, mother to Ben and Jo, two weeks old.

Positioning twins at the breast when feeding them together is not an easy skill to achieve, but practice does improve things. It's probably more important that you are comfortable before you start, which means having your back and shoulders well supported and then resting the babies on pillows until the right height is achieved.

WINDING YOUR BABY

Whether you breastfeed or bottlefeed, your baby may need winding in order to bring up any air that she has swallowed while feeding. We all tend to get rather worked up about trapped wind and blame it for any cries of anguish our babies emit over the first three months (before teething becomes the scapegoat), although a number of childcare experts have noted that many babies seem to be just as happy (or miserable) whether they've been burped or not. Still, it is always reassuring for us parents to hear a resounding belch after a feed and giving your baby a rub or gentle pat on the back isn't going to do any harm and may be doing some good. The key is not to become hysterical if you don't get any action after several minutes of working at it – and certainly don't insist on stopping a feed halfway to try and produce a burp. Some babies (especially breastfed ones) are simply not windy.

HOW TO DO IT

After a feed, put your baby over your shoulder or sit her on your knee supported by one forearm. With the other arm, firmly stroke your baby's back in an upwards motion or give her some gentle pats.

COMBINING BREAST AND BOTTLE

Yes it can be done – and it can be the best compromise for many mums who need some freedom from feeding to work or rest. Perhaps you are happy to feed your baby all day, but want to slip off to bed early and leave your partner to do the late evening feeds. Or maybe you need to work in the day, but want to continue breastfeeding in the morning and evening. All of this is possible, as long as you have got breastfeeding well established first. As a rule of thumb, avoid introducing a bottle until your baby is about six weeks old. If you do so before then she may well be confused by the different action that sucking from a bottle requires, and may reject the breast in favour of the bottle, which requires far less effort on her part!

If you have been breastfeeding exclusively until now, you'll notice that your breasts will be full and rather tender at the time of the bottlefeed for the first couple of days. Don't be tempted to express the milk to relieve the tenderness as that will only stimulate your milk supply in the same way feeding your baby would and you'll continue to get the same problem. Instead try to relieve any tenderness with a cold flannel and rest assured that it will not continue.

There is no reason why you shouldn't swap as many feeds as you like for a bottlefeed. Many women who return to work keep only the morning and evening breastfeed and find that works well, though for a few the milk supply does begin to dwindle somewhat, especially if they are only breastfeeding in the evening.

WEANING FROM THE BREAST COMPLETELY

If you know that you will need to switch from breast to bottlefeeding at some point in the future then it is often worth introducing a bottle at around eight weeks for one feed a day, just so your baby is used to it and there isn't a fuss when you need to go back to work, say. Most babies, if they had their way, would continue to enjoy the comfort of breastfeeding for nine months or more – so if you have other plans you may want to give your baby this little taster of what is to come before she gets too stuck in her ways!

When you do decide to wean, allow yourself a couple of weeks to do it comfortably, and (as mentioned above) never express milk to reduce the pressure on your breasts. If they are very painful then you could relieve them by squeezing out a little milk, but certainly not a feed's worth or you will only stimulate the supply once more. Wait until your breasts are comfortable at that feed time before you try to drop another feed. This will usually take about three days, so, assuming your baby is having four feeds a day, it should take just under two weeks to complete the process. Be sure to give your baby plenty of cuddles and attention and allow her to adopt a comfort object if that helps her to settle.

Some babies, once offered a bottle, actually decide that they prefer that type of feeding and reject the breast themselves, while others become very independent at nine months or so and decide they've had enough and would prefer a beaker. If that's case, you simply have to follow.

I am desperate to wean my baby off the breast, but he will not take a bottle. I'm at the end of my tether.

Gina, mother to Daniel, three months old.

There are several things you can try. First, experiment with different teats. Try the orthodontic-shaped teats which look a bit flatter than the standard ones, and experiment with varying speeds of teat too. Secondly get someone else to offer your baby the bottle. If he can smell milk from your breasts he will be less inclined to try the bottle. Finally, don't despair. Some babies will not take a bottle but instead graduate straight to a beaker. Look for a variety with a soft chewable spout and see if he will take that.

Q

I've been breastfeeding until now, but I've started introducing a bottle to my baby recently. The problem is she cries when every bottle is finished, however much is in it. It has got to the stage where she is drinking 8oz (250ml) at every feed whereas my friends' babies only have 6oz (170ml).

Emma, mother to Sophie, 14 weeks old.

If you think your baby is genuinely hungry you could offer her the milk designed for hungrier babies instead (see What you'll need, page 78). However, your baby may be just missing the comfort of sucking for an extended period at the breast. Bottlefeeding generally is quicker than breastfeeding so the feeds are over and done with more quickly than she is used to. You could try distracting her as soon as the bottle is finished, perhaps with a favourite teddy or blanket, and try to give her as many cuddles and close contact with you as possible so that she still feels secure.

With regards to the amount she is drinking, remember that your baby's size (i.e. her weight) is more relevant than her age when it comes to determining how much she needs. The age guidelines on the sides of tins of formula should be treated as a general guide only. Pay attention to her weight gain. If she seems to be putting on a lot of weight then you should consider reducing the amount she has at each feed.

Q

*I am bottlefeeding my baby exclusively and have heard that I
need to offer him water as well. Do I need to sterilize the
water bottles in the same way as the milk ones?*

Stephanie, mother to Charlie, three months old.

You are right, a bottlefed baby does need to be offered
water between feeds, as formula milk does not contain
the same thirst-quenching properties as breastmilk. With
regards to sterilizing, it is advisable to sterilize everything that your baby puts into his mouth for the first six
months at least. Boiled, cooled water doesn't pose the
same risk of infection as milk, but it's better to be on the
safe side. (Don't offer your baby mineral water as these
bottled waters generally contain more salts and minerals
than are good for your baby's immature kidneys.)

A

Q

*I have eczema and I want to protect my baby from it as
much as I can, however I would also like to give her the odd
formula feed. Will that increase her chances of getting
eczema?*

Ann, mother to Olivia, six weeks old.

If there is a history of eczema in the family, avoiding
cow's milk in the first six months may help to prevent
your baby developing it. Perhaps you could consider
expressing milk to give her in a bottle or trying her on a
soya-based milk instead.

INTRODUCING SOLIDS

WHEN TO DO IT

Researchers are always looking at when is the best time to introduce your baby to something more exciting than milk alone – with the result that parents of more than one child often find they are being given completely different advice for child number two than they had for child number one. I think this goes to show that perhaps it's best just to follow your own baby's lead and your own instincts – you can't go far wrong.

The general idea is to avoid introducing anything other than milk for as long as your baby is happy, in order to reduce the risk of sensitizing your child to allergies. So, if at five months your baby is still happy on milk alone that's fine – there is no need to rush to the blender with a handful of carrots. Offering solids to babies under three months should not be necessary and should be avoided, but by six months most babies will be looking for something a bit more interesting than milk alone, and may even start trying to grab things off your dinner plate if you don't offer them some of their own.

Four months is therefore probably about the right time to start thinking about purées – especially if your baby seems to be dissatisfied with milk alone and maybe is even waking up in the night feeling peckish.

WHAT YOU NEED

- ❀ Small spoon – preferably plastic
- ❀ Small bowl
- ❀ Fork to mash soft foods, such as banana
- ❀ A sieve can be used to purée vegetables after cooking
- ❀ A blender is useful for quick purées
- ❀ Bibs
- ❀ Chair for your baby – this could be the car seat or baby bouncing chair.

HOW TO START

At around four months your baby will probably be ready to start experimenting with solids. The golden rules are:

- ❀ Start at a time when your baby is peckish but not starving (perhaps in the middle of a milk feed at lunchtime if you can interrupt her).
- ❀ Introduce just one new food at a time (so you can assess which ones cause an upset).
- ❀ Remember that your baby may only want a teaspoon at first.
- ❀ Don't force it (if she doesn't want it, try again another day).
- ❀ Only introduce new foods at lunchtime (to avoid bedtime angst if it disagrees with her).

Be patient and be prepared for plenty of mess! As much food may seem to come out of your baby's mouth as went in to begin with and your baby may well cry in between mouthfuls. This isn't to indicate her disgust at baby rice, but is simply because she is used to her food (milk) coming in a continuous stream and doesn't like to wait while you reload the spoon!

Good foods to start with are:

Rice cereals mixed with breast or formula milk
Puréed cooked vegetables such as carrots, green beans, peas, potato
Puréed fruit, such as cooked apple, pears, bananas
(Do *not* add salt or sugar to any food)

Do not yet give:

Wheat-based foods (including bread)
Dairy products (including cow's milk)
Eggs
Citrus fruits
Nuts
Fatty foods
Chillies

These can cause allergic reactions. Wait until your baby is six months.

Don't make mealtimes a performance, with you turning every spoonful into a fast running train or diving aeroplane. Your baby probably won't eat any more and in fact may refuse food just to enjoy the show. When he doesn't want any more, just call an end to the meal.

Sarah, health visitor.

AROUND SIX MONTHS ONWARDS

Once your baby has got used to the spoon and seems to enjoy her purées you can start to increase the amount you give her and gradually make the texture lumpier. Let your baby be the guide when it comes to portion size, and you won't go wrong. Now you can begin to move from having solid food at just one mealtime a day, to having some solids at two and then three mealtimes a day. At the same time you can gradually reduce the milk feeds, but make sure your baby still has half a litre (one pint) of milk a day and offer her a drink of water or diluted natural fruit juice with meals.

At six months you can begin to give your baby some of the food that you have yourself (as long as you don't add salt or sugar). Just mash or sieve a small amount. This will help your baby get accustomed to eating like the rest of the family and should avoid her becoming too picky, if you're lucky, although you should still leave out nuts and greasy or spicy food.

Foods to add now:	**Still avoid:**
Meat	Greasy or spicy food
Poultry	Nuts
Pulses	Bran cereals
Bread	Sugary food or drinks
Pasta	
Egg yolk (cooked solid)	
Yogurt	
You can also use cow's milk for mixing food such as cereal or mashed potato.	

NINE MONTHS TO A YEAR

Offer your baby meals in pieces rather than mashed up so she can pick them up with her fingers. There's no reason why she shouldn't now be able to join in when you all tuck into a roast dinner or a casserole and fruit crumble. Start to give your baby a spoon to hold so that she gets used to the idea of using cutlery, even if the food doesn't yet make it to her mouth!

Foods to add now:

Fish
Sandwiches
Sticks of raw carrot, cucumber and apple.
At 12 months you can offer your baby full-cream cow's milk to drink instead of formula or breastmilk. She still needs half a litre (one pint) of milk a day.

Still avoid:

Nuts, including peanuts or peanut butter (Recent research suggests that introducing peanuts too early could trigger nut allergies. Also, whole nuts can cause a baby to choke.)
Fatty, sugary and salty foods – aim for a healthy diet

MAKING LIFE EASIER

In the early days of solids you may begin to feel that you have a closer relationship with your blender than with your baby. Chopping, cooking and whizzing up purées three times a day can get tiresome pretty quickly, so try to make life a bit easier by cooking in bulk. When you get a chance, cook up a quantity of vegetables and fruits and freeze them either in small freezer containers or in ice cube trays. Then you only have to remember to take a few cubes out of the freezer each morning to have a day's meals to hand. Also, take heart in the fact that this stage only lasts a couple of months and you can soon get away with mashing up the family's dinners. Try not to fall into the trap of always preparing something specially for your baby or you may find that she never tucks in with the rest of you at mealtimes.

Although the range of commercially prepared baby food is getting better and better, it is preferable to use it only when you are out and about or for emergencies, rather than on a daily basis. Nothing beats freshly made food with no additives – and giving your baby food you have made yourself will accustom her to your cooking and family meals. Make life easier for yourself by cooking in bulk and using frozen vegetables (they may be fresher than the vegetables you've had in your larder for a few days). Desserts can be simply a mashed banana or, when she's six months, a little pot of fromage frais. You'll find you save money too!

FEEDING SOLIDS TO TWINS

When it comes to feeding your twins solids, sit them both in their baby chairs or car seats in front of you and just use one bowl and spoon to feed both of them. Trying to juggle two spoons and two bowls is best left to circus performers.

Once your baby starts to feed himself and eat finger foods, lay out some newspaper or a plastic mat under his chair to make cleaning up easier afterwards.

Dawn, mother to Thomas, one year old.

When your baby is eight months or so, give him a spoon to hold while you feed him. This encourages babies to become active with cutlery and eventually to feed themselves.

Jayne, nanny.

Q

My baby is only three months old, but he is still waking at night. Do you think giving him solids would help him to sleep through?

Hilary, mother to Ross, three months old.

If your baby has been sleeping through the night, but has recently taken to waking, then it could be that he is hungry – especially if he doesn't seem satisfied after his milk feeds during the day. However, if your baby has always been a poor sleeper then giving him solids will probably make no difference at all. Introducing solids too early can put a strain on a baby's immature digestive system and certain foods can even cause allergies, so it really is best to wait until he is four months old if you can.

Do I have to sterilize the bowl and spoon I use for feeding my baby?

Claire, mother to Isaac, four months old.

Cleanliness is important so your feeding equipment should be as clean as possible and the spoon should ideally be sterilized for the first couple of months. If you are sterilizing bottles and teats anyway then it isn't too difficult to just throw in a few spoons. If you have a dishwasher your bowls and spoons will be getting a thorough hot wash so you needn't be so concerned.

Perhaps more important than sterilizing the implements involved is the storage of the food itself. Don't leave food standing at room temperature as it is a breeding ground for germs – and never keep half-eaten foods for another day as germs will have been passed to the food from your baby's mouth via the spoon. If you don't think your baby will eat a dish in just one sitting then divide it into smaller portions before you offer it to him.

From day one I always dressed Alyssa at mealtimes in a plastic bib with sleeves so she was completely covered. It didn't take long for her to associate it with food being on the way and it meant that when she was older, and feeding herself in a very messy fashion, she never made a fuss about putting on the overall.

Sheila, mother to Alyssa, one year old.

Q

I want to bring my baby up to be a vegetarian like myself, is there anything I should know when I start to give her a solid diet?

Katrina, mother to Amanda, four months old.

If you include milk products and eggs in your vegetarian diet then it will be easy to ensure your baby has a good diet. Dairy products provide calcium and protein for growth and vitamins A, B12 and D, while egg yolks provide iron. For the first couple of months on solids, simple fruit and vegetable purées and baby rice are all your baby needs. At six months plus you can offer your baby wholegrain cereals, pasta, rice, tofu and other soya-based products for protein. Also give plenty of leafy green vegetables and broccoli to ensure she has all the vitamins she needs. If your baby eats well, she shouldn't need to have any sort of vitamin supplement.

A

Survival tips

Deciding how you will feed your baby needn't be a black or white matter. You can combine bottlefeeds with breastfeeds – as long as you wait six weeks until your baby is well settled at the breast.

✿

Breastfeed your baby if you can and it suits you, but don't let it bother you if you can't. It is just as important that you are happy.

✿

Get as much help as you want from the health professionals to make sure you and your baby have got the hang of breastfeeding.

✿

Introduce solids only when your baby is ready – around four or five months is usual.

✿

Do not make dinner times a battle. If your baby has had enough then so be it.

✿

Avoid dairy products until your baby is six months old.

✿

Never add salt or sugar to your baby's food.

4

Crying

Sometimes it seems that your baby
purposefully lulled you into a false
sense of security in the hospital (when
all he seemed to do was sleep and
make a quiet whimper), before coming
home to reveal his true colours – and
lung capacity!

Few things will make a new parent
more anxious than the sound of their
baby crying. Yes, Mother Nature
deserves some sort of design award for
the effect that cry has on a mum and dad. Within a few seconds of it
starting, a mother's heart rate is quicker, her blood pressure has risen
and she will not relax until her baby is happy once more. Both parents
may find themselves getting tense, even angry, and are soon snapping
at one another too. It can be hard to cope with – especially in the early
weeks – but rest assured that it does get better. Your baby's crying will
soon become easier to interpret and he will be easier to pacify as the
months go by. In the meantime, stay as calm as you can, and try some
of the tried and tested comforting techniques given here.

IN THE EARLY DAYS

Crying is your baby's way of telling you that he wants something. He may not be too sure what that is – he just knows that he's uncomfortable in some way and will voice his protestations until he feels comfortable once again. The problem is that, in the early days, while you are still getting to know each other, you will not be sure what it is he wants, and sometimes will have to try at least three different things before you discover the problem.

WHY IS HE CRYING?

There are a certain number of common reasons for a baby's discomfort that will cause him to cry.

Hunger   In the early weeks this is the usual cause of your baby's tears, so always offer a crying baby a breast or bottle and see if it pacifies him. If you are breastfeeding then you may find your baby wants to feed quite frequently on some days, and maybe most of the time in the evenings. Do not worry about this (see Feeding your baby, chapter 3), you cannot overfeed a breastfed baby and there will always be some milk in the breast for him.

Pain   If you have offered your baby some milk and that hasn't calmed him, then it could be that he is in pain. In time you will notice that a cry of pain is quite different to any other, but for now it is worth checking that his nappy and clothes are comfortable and trying to bring up any wind that might be giving him tummy ache.

Loneliness   Your baby loves being close to you as it makes him feel warm and secure, so if he gets upset after being left in a crib or Moses basket for a while, it may be that he just fancies a cuddle.

Don't worry that this is an early sign of your baby's manipulative skills if he demands to be held. By picking him up and giving him the comfort he craves, you are not 'giving in', but are making him feel secure and content. In many cultures a baby is held and carried almost all day long.

Cold Babies are very sensitive to changes in temperature and cannot regulate their own body heat as we can. If it is a bit chilly then try giving him another blanket or another layer of clothes and cuddle him until he warms up. If your baby always cries when you change his nappy or take his clothes off for a bath you may have assumed that this was because he was feeling cold. However, many young babies don't like their skin exposed to the air (whatever its temperature) because they miss the comforting contact with their clothes.

Fear This is quite obvious to spot – your baby will react with tears to something that comes as a surprise or is alien to him. It might be simply that you turned on a bright light, sneezed loudly or appeared suddenly, but it is enough to frighten someone who is only just getting to grips with the world. A cuddle will normally pacify him if this is the case.

Tiredness If you have checked all the above and your baby is still fretful, then it could well be that he is simply tired. When we adults feel tired we know that the best thing is to go to bed and sleep, but for a baby it's not always that simple. There are times when a baby will cry because he is tired, but well-meaning parents will just not give him a chance to sleep. They try to jig him around to cheer him up or put so much effort into making him happy again that he finds it quite exhausting and cries even louder. Sometimes the best thing you can do for your baby is simply put him down in his crib, and leave him to it. You'll probably find that he is fast asleep within ten minutes of leaving him.

Q

My mother has been staying to help me since my baby was born and is amazed that I feed her every time she cries. She says babies need to be left to cry sometimes to exercise their lungs. I can't believe that is true though.

Anna, mother to Colette, three weeks old.

Previous generations often took a firmer line with babies than we do today, and, with more emphasis on routine and 'discipline' did not believe in feeding on demand or giving a baby immediate comfort – to prevent the baby from 'ruling the roost'. It is not true that a baby cries to exercise her lungs. She is human. She cries because she wants something and, as her mother, you are biologically programmed to respond. Follow your instincts, it is quite likely that she does want feeding, or if not, the comfort of sucking.

A

HOW TO COMFORT YOUR BABY

There are times when there seems to be no reason for your baby's crying – but then we all have bad days when we just fancy a grumble. When you have tried treating him for all of the above to no avail, just concentrate on calming him as best you can. Close physical contact is the best way of comforting a crying baby. Put yourself in his position – for nine months or so he has been in one nicely regulated environment where he did not have to want for food or warmth, was kept quite closely confined and was rocked about whenever you moved. Now he is in a new world where he spends periods of time further away from you than ever before and is often kept waiting for his milk supply. It is hardly surprising that he craves constant human contact, or anything that reminds him of his more familiar little home in the womb. Here are some techniques for providing that contact:

Rocking   Your baby was used to being rocked in the womb as you went about your daily business. Whenever he is upset, pick him up and hold him close to you, rocking him by walking around the room. According to researchers, rocking has to be quite fast to soothe a baby – ideally about 60 rocks per minute – so a gentle rocking of a crib is less successful than a stroll around the house. Some babies like to be rocked from side to side, others up and down – try out different techniques with your baby, but don't be too vigorous.

Use a sling or shawl   Carrying your baby in a sling will offer him the warmth, security and movement he enjoys, but will leave your arms free to carry on as normal – well, almost. This can be particularly useful in the crotchety evening time when you have a meal to prepare but your baby will not settle.

Singing   Experiment with different types of singing and music to see what works for your baby. Some babies like a Brahm's lullaby, whereas others would prefer something more lively. Different babies like different pitches and rhythms so if you find one which calms your baby, stick to it!

Rhythmic sounds   Life in the womb is quite noisy and, once born, many babies seem to be soothed by even quite loud rhythmic sounds such as a vacuum cleaner, a washing machine, a hair dryer or the hum of a fan.

> I remember keeping the hair dryer on for at least half an hour at a time as it seemed to keep Lily asleep – and I was desperate to have a rest myself. My old work colleagues were quite amused to hear the hair dryer every time they phoned me!
>
> Karen, mother to Lily, one year old.

Massage   This seems to work a treat for many babies, although it never worked with mine – probably just because I lack a gentle touch, but they never lay still for long enough! You may find a class that teaches massage for babies or you can learn the techniques from a book, but simple stroking and patting of his back or tummy is probably just as effective as anything more complex. Just let your maternal (or paternal) instincts to pat and smooth take over and you won't go wrong.

   The golden rules of baby massage are to take your time, keep him warm, use some almond oil on your hands to moisturize your baby's skin and let your hands glide gently over his body. It is best to practise this at a time when your baby is not frantic and crying, then see if it will work as a soother when he is.

Swaddling   This is an age-old method that works well with many
babies by making them feel confined and secure. Fold a cellular
blanket or flannel cot sheet into a triangle and lay it underneath
your baby with the point of the triangle at his feet. Bring one side
over his body and tuck it under his body on the opposite side, then
repeat with the other side so that your baby's arms are enclosed
and the blanket is quite snug. Fold the tip of the blanket upwards
and tuck it into a fold to keep it secure.

Often a new Mum will phone in saying her baby will not sleep or stop
crying and she has been feeding him for hours and hours — which can
be exhausting when you've just had a baby. I often go and see them,
swaddle the baby up tightly and put him out of earshot for ten
minutes, in his crib where we know he's safe. Nine times out of ten the
baby will be asleep when I go and check.

Corinne, midwife.

Take him out in the car   The rhythmical movement of the car has a
magical effect on a baby – if only we did not have to stop at traffic
lights or come home at all. Your baby may stop crying while you
cruise around town, but is quite likely to start again as soon as you
have parked outside your house so this isn't the best technique to
try in the middle of the night – unless you are desperate.

Go for a walk with the pram   This usually works after a while,
although you may have to suffer critical looks from passers-by for
the first few minutes while your baby yells and thrashes in the pram.
The advantage of this technique is that once your baby drops off to
sleep and you come home, you may be able to bring the pram
inside and allow him to carry on sleeping.

I find Martin is much better at calming Tilly than I am. I'm sure she likes the firm confident way he handles her.

Rebecca, mother to Tilly, three weeks old.

I still can't recognize the difference between my baby's cries so I feel really inadequate. It also means that I'm feeding my baby constantly because that seems to settle her. Am I doing the wrong thing?

Eleanor, mother to Ruth, three weeks old.

There is no need to feel inadequate. It takes a long time to get to know another human being and recognize their body language and cries. In the meantime, while your baby is a newborn, you are doing the right thing to respond by offering food. You would soon find out if that was not the problem! The next time your baby cries and you are unsure as to whether or not she can really be hungry, try comforting her in another way first, such as rocking or singing, but go back to offering food if that seems to be the only thing that settles her. At this stage it is best to let your baby guide you with regard to feeding, although if she is bottlefed keep an eye on her weight and the centile charts your health visitor or doctor will show you. As your baby gets older and the gaps between feeds increase, you'll find it easier to relax about feeding and will learn to recognize the different cries of frustration, boredom, pain and so on.

Q

Am I spoiling my baby by picking her up immediately when she cries?

Ann, mother to Poppy, three weeks old.

Research has shown that babies who are comforted quickly when they cry, generally (and perhaps conversely) turn into toddlers who are more confident, independent and cry less than their contemporaries. Your baby needs to know that you are there for her when she needs you. If she is confident that you will be, then she will be prepared to be that bit more independent at other times. If she never knows whether you will come and pick her up or not, she will, understandably, stay closer and become more clingy and demanding.

Do not, however, tie yourself into knots and leap down ladders just to get to your baby the instant she cries. If you are doing something that cannot be left for a minute, then she will just have to wait – as long as you are sure that she can come to no harm in the meantime.

We ended up buying two types of sling. I know it sounds extravagant, but the shawl style of sling kept Helen closer and more snug and seemed to soothe her better when she was upset in the evenings, whereas the standard type of baby carrier was better for going out and about – especially when Paul was going to carry her because he didn't like to walk around in a shawl!

Julia, mother to Helen, seven months old.

My baby is very fretful, but if I give her a dummy to settle her will it stop her from feeding enough from me? I'm worried that she will get all her sucking satisfaction from that.

Emma, mother to Florence, two weeks old.

Experts seem somewhat undecided on this one. Some believe that a new baby may not bother to feed as much as she should if she can get her satisfaction from sucking on a dummy, whereas others say that if a baby is hungry she will not be interested in a dummy and will cry until some milk is provided. I think you have to treat each baby as an individual and keep a careful eye on your baby if you decide to offer her a dummy to settle her. As long as you do not fall into the trap of offering your baby a dummy every time she cries, rather than looking to find the real reason why she is upset, then a dummy will not do your baby any harm.

I live by myself and found that the colicky evenings were very hard. Luckily I had a good set of friends and I used to have a different one around every evening to pass Lucy over to. Having a chum there took my mind off the crying and having another pair of arms was so useful.

Maggie, mother to Lucy, four months old.

THREE TO FOUR WEEKS OLD – THE ARRIVAL OF COLIC

For many parents, everything goes swimmingly until their baby reaches three or four weeks old, then it all seems to go horribly wrong. Suddenly their baby starts to get really fractious and tearful in the evening and nothing seems to settle him. Soon they realize that a pattern is developing and their darling boy is now screaming every evening from about five o'clock until as late as nine or ten in the evening. Welcome to the world of colic.

Colic is the term given to this sanity-threatening pattern of crying because it is very often put down to the baby having tummy ache. This is because one of the typical signs of a colicky baby is that he will pull his legs up to his tummy while he is crying, suggesting that it is his tummy giving him some pain and making him cry. However there are also plenty of babies who develop this awful evening crying, but never bring their legs up at all. If you suspect your baby may have colic, here are the typical signs to look out for, although every baby is somewhat different.

✿ The pattern starts at around three or four weeks old.
✿ Crying usually starts after feeding in the later afternoon.
✿ Your baby is inconsolable and cannot be settled in the normal ways, although some things seem to work for a few minutes.
✿ Crying can turn to screaming.
✿ The crying session will last at least two or three hours.
✿ It seems to be a daily occurrence.
✿ The baby may pass wind.
✿ He may pull his knees up and clench his fists.
✿ He may think he wants to feed then reject it, doze off momentarily or be sick afterwards.

The good news is that although it feels like living hell at the time, colic will strangely and miraculously disappear by the time your baby is 11–12 weeks old. You might suddenly notice that you have had a night off from the usual game of pacing up and down and passing the baby to and fro, then a few days later, you realize that he has not done it for a couple of nights – and soon you are home and dry.

WHAT CAUSES COLIC?

The jury is still out on this one and, to be honest, most parents of a colicky baby do not care too much what the reason is, they just want it to stop. However, these are the current trends of thought on the matter:

Excess wind Many colicky babies do seem to suffer from excess wind, but seeing as they are spending all evening yelling and swallowing vast amounts of air as they do so it is hard to say for sure whether it is a cause or an effect. Some people do find that giving their babies an antacid medicine such as Infacol does help, but others doubt whether it has any effect at all.

Tummy ache, triggered by something in the milk True, babies do get upset tummies as a result of food that the mother has eaten or something in the formula milk, but it seems unlikely that it could cause regular evening crying unless it is something that you eat every day. Some breastfeeding mothers find cutting out dairy products from their diet has an effect so you could always give that a go. After all, doing without a piece of cheese or milk is a small price to pay for an evening without crying.

Smokers in the household Cigarette smoke does seem to increase the likelihood of colic and exacerbate it, but does not explain why babies in non-smoking houses also suffer from colic.

A tired and tense parent If you are exhausted and irritable after a long day, this will be transmitted to your baby and may make him irritable too. However, this still does not seem a completely adequate explanation. What is more likely is that once the crying starts, your anxiety makes it worse.

An immature digestive system Babies need time for their gut and/or nervous system to mature and the crying could just be an extreme symptom of this. Your baby's internal workings suddenly have to cope with milk being pumped in at frequent intervals and, like many complex machines, it can take time before everything is up and running satisfactorily.

Sensory overload At around three weeks old (when colic most often starts) babies begin to become much more aware of what is around them – and there is an awful lot to take in, in any household. It may be that they become overwhelmed by all the noises, smells and sights they have absorbed during the day and, by the early evening, can only cry in desperation. Supporters of this theory then argue that by the time a baby reaches three or four months (when colic usually ends), he is able to block out a lot of the hubbub that occurs around him and cope with it better.

Reductions in maternal hormones The levels of the hormones your baby received from you in the womb are decreasing at this time and it is thought this may cause spasms.

Basically no one has a definitive explanation for colic – and it seems likely that it is the result of more than one factor. So where does that leave you? Still stuck in the house with a screaming baby of course, feeling none the wiser and getting ever more frantic. Stay calm, and follow the tips on the next page.

WHAT TO DO – AND HOW TO SAVE YOUR SANITY

✿ Try to comfort your baby using any of the suggestions given on page 102. They may or may not work, but at least you feel like you are doing something.

✿ When you hold him, keep trying different positions until you find one that works. Colicky babies seem to particularly like positions where there is some gentle pressure on their stomach. Try holding him flat on his stomach along your arm or knees, and rubbing his back gently, but firmly.

✿ Put him in a shawl or sling so that you can rock him and keep him close to you, but still have your arms free to get on or at least eat some dinner – albeit standing up!

✿ Share the burden with your partner – or someone else. A crying baby can drive the most level-headed of people to distraction – especially when it continues for over two hours. Pass the baby to your partner and take turns to have a break, ideally out of earshot of the screams. Take a long, hot bath with some music in the background to drown the noise.

✿ Forget everything except coping with the crying and making sure you eat. Reread the tips on page 32 for coping at home with a new baby and make sure you stick to them!

✿ When all else fails and you are at the end of your tether, take some time out and put your baby in his cot where he is safe. Close the door and move as far out of earshot as you can, even if it is just for ten minutes.

✿ However difficult it is living with a colicky baby, try to remember that it is only a phase and not an indication of how your evenings will be forever more. By the time your baby is four months old, the nights pacing the livingroom floor should be well and truly over and by the time he is six months you will find it hard to remember what all the fuss was about – well maybe … .

Q

I'm a single parent with a baby who has colic every evening so I find it very hard. I do not have anyone to pass him over to or anyone to sound off to when I am feeling desperate. I often find it hard to even eat an evening meal as I am carrying him round all of the time. I feel like I am going out of my mind.

Laura, mother to Jo, eight weeks old.

Coping with colic is bad enough, but coping on your own is doubly tough – you are doing a wonderful job. If you do not have anyone to hand the baby over to so that you can have a break occasionally, then why not take him out in the car or pram and go to see a friend or just have a walk? The motion may soothe your baby to sleep for a while, and you will at least have a chance to walk off your tension or offload onto a friendly shoulder. Staying in with your baby alone will end up in you becoming so tense that your baby is sure to pick up on it and become more agitated. It is a vicious circle.

With regards to making something to eat, invest in a sling to carry him while you cook, or prepare something while he sleeps during the day.

When Chelsea had colic I used to put the television on with subtitles (I couldn't hear it above the crying!), put her in the sling and sway from side to side in front of the television. It eventually sent her to sleep and watching television helped to take my mind off it all.

Jenny, mother to Chelsea, five months old.

Q

My baby has had colic for the past three weeks and sometimes I really feel like hurling her against the wall. I know it is an awful thing to say, and I am sure that I wouldn't really do it, but sometimes I would do anything to make the crying stop.

Steven, father to Lucy, six weeks old.

You are not the only parent to feel like this. Both mums and dads find themselves really pushed to the limit when their baby has colic – and it is hardly surprising. The baby seems to carry on thriving regardless of the evening tension, whereas the parents soon find the cracks starting to show.

If you really think that you might hurt the baby, then you must tell a professional, such as your health visitor or doctor, and get some practical help looking after the baby – maybe some counselling too. It is important that you do not let things get out of control. The moment you begin not to trust yourself, go immediately to your partner or a neighbour and hand over the baby until you can calm down.

If, however, you think you are essentially in control, there are other ways to help you get through this difficult period. First, take regular breaks from the crying, even if it is only by putting in some earplugs while you pace the room. Secondly, try taking regular exercise either on your own during the day or by taking the baby for a brisk walk – it will help to lessen the tension and aggression you are feeling. Thirdly, talk about how you are feeling to your partner, a friend or a professional.

 A

Q

My baby cries every evening. She is pacified by breastfeeding for a while, but then she just brings the whole lot up. Could this be colic and what can I do?

Sally, mother to Sophie, seven weeks old.

It probably is – especially if this is happening every evening and she cannot be pacified. Many babies with colic think they are hungry and root for food while they are crying, but although this calms them for a while, it can actually make the colic worse afterwards. The fact that she is bringing the milk up again is a sign that her stomach is either upset or she did not need the milk in the first place – either way try to calm her in some other way than feeding. Try some of the other techniques given above, and consider offering her a dummy instead of a nipple. Do also keep an eye on her weight gain to make sure that she is keeping enough milk down.

 A

FROM THREE MONTHS TO SIX MONTHS

By the time your baby reaches three months, his crying should have become much easier to cope with. Usually colic has come to an end and you are, believe it or not, in some kind of routine. Instead of your baby suddenly launching into heart-rending yells which do not subside until his demands are met, you may notice that you are being given a little bit of warning that he is not 100 per cent happy which gives you time to act before the crying reaches a crescendo. Your baby will have a special little moany, whimpery, grumbling cry that says, 'Mum I could do with something a bit more interesting to play with now' or 'I think I might be getting a little bit tired/peckish/hot' and so on.

Of course every now and then you will still get a real ear-bender of a yell, but it is more likely to be one of pain or frustration and is much easier to interpret.

Your baby still needs you as much as ever though and will still need and want as much reassurance and close contact as before. In fact there may come a point, at around four or five months, when you think he is so demanding and is grumbling so often that you cannot imagine ever getting anything done. This is usually because he is becoming more and more wakeful and alert and needs much more entertaining than before, yet is still not mature enough to be able to sit and play by himself. This is the time when a sling or backcarrier, a bouncing chair and a baby bouncer can come into their own. Your baby can then watch what you are up to and feel that he is being involved, without you having to carry him around in your arms all day.

FROM SIX MONTHS ONWARDS

You will be relieved to hear that babies cry a lot less from this point on. He is becoming strong and dexterous enough to sit up and play with any toys you surround him with and so will become easier to keep amused. Now the main causes of crying are quite different to those of the first six months:

Helplessness   There is so much that your baby wants to do, but he can't yet physically manage. He can't follow you wherever you go and he can't reach every toy he wants. In the weeks before they start to crawl, many babies reach a peak of frustration and sit crying or shouting loudly, simply because they cannot get to where they want to be. Soon, however, crawling comes and opens up a whole new world of entertainment for him – and constant worry for you!

Fears Your baby has become used to his own little world now. He recognizes the familiar faces and the routines of breakfast, lunch, dinner, bath, bed and so on. This all helps to make him feel secure and happy 90 per cent of the time, but means he may also be very fearful of a very new situation or a new face invading his space. You may know that your Aunty Barbara only wants to give your little boy a cuddle, but he is not at all sure what is going on. The best thing you can do is respect his feelings and do not try to force him into a situation he will not be happy in – then, in time, he will become more confident. Many of these fears are Nature's way of keeping your baby safe as he becomes more mobile and runs the risk of straying too far from your side. Some fears may seem completely irrational to you, but then you probably have some strange fears too, so try to see his point of view.

Frustration and anger Once your baby becomes mobile, the tears from helplessness decrease, but are replaced those stemming from anger and frustration. He wants to go out and explore everything around him, without any regard for whether or not sticking something new and exciting in his mouth will result in a trip to the hospital emergency department. You, on the other hand, are far more aware of the possible consequences of his actions and spend a lot of your time thwarting his attempts to discover what the fire/fridge/electricity/bleach and so on taste like. It takes a while for a baby to learn about 'No' and even longer to understand why you are saying it so there will be plenty of tears along the way.

Whenever Charlie gets grumpy I put him in the baby bouncer on the doorframe and it cheers him up. I think he is so active and wakeful he would love to be upright more of the time than his body will yet allow him to be!

Karen, mother to Charlie, five months old.

For two weeks, when he was six months old, George sat on the floor and moaned and moaned. Then he started to crawl and suddenly cried much less and became much happier.

Emma, mother to George, nine months old.

My baby seems to cry at the slightest strange noise or tumble whereas my friend's baby seems to take far more in her stride. Could it be because I've been too soft with him?

Clare, mother to Joshua, seven months old.

For fear of sounding like a broken record, all babies are different. Your baby, at this moment in time, is a little bit less tolerant of certain setbacks than your friend's baby – that is just the way he is. That does not mean that he will be 'soft' forever more however, he just needs time to develop his confidence at his own pace and it is unlikely to be the result of your parenting skills. Help him and comfort him now as much as he needs and forget any ideas of trying to 'toughen him up' – he will develop at his own pace.

Q

My baby seems to cry far more frequently than others still, and I am not sure why.

Chantal, mother to Eddie, eight months old.

If he does seem to cry a lot every day, and you are sure it is not just because he is feeling a little out of sorts at the moment (due to a cold or tummy upset perhaps) then it could be that something specific is bothering him, but you are finding it hard to distinguish what it is. To make it easier to pinpoint the problem it can help to keep a diary of his crying spells, noting exactly when he cried, what you think you caused it and what comforted him. For example, 'After lunch, Eddie started crying when he was sitting on the floor playing with his toys, but he stopped when I picked him up.' After a few days you may notice a pattern where he is crying mostly out of frustration, anger or maybe hunger – then you will be able to take steps to prevent him becoming so frustrated/hungry etc. (You may also find that he becomes more settle once he is mobile.)

A

I have put up a playpen in the kitchen and filled it with toys so that Molly can play happily and safely while I work and she doesn't feel abandoned.

Suzie, mother to Molly, six months old.

Survival tips

Remember that all babies cry – it's their only way of getting your attention and telling you something is wrong.

The more quickly you respond to your baby, the more confident he will feel and become.

Most crying in the first few weeks is due to hunger. If that does not seem to be the cause, check whether he could be in pain, too hot or cold, tired, or just in need of a cuddle.

Walking with your baby, holding him close, singing and other rhythmic sounds are all tried and tested methods of soothing.

If your baby develops a pattern of crying every evening, it is probably colic, and all you can do is weather the storm until is stops – at around 11 weeks.

Do not suffer alone if your baby cries a lot – get as much support as you can.

Take heart, your baby will cry less as he gets older.

5

Development – the major milestones

Every baby is different and develops at a different rate – and the speed with which they do so is no indication of their potential to be a rocket scientist (or not) in the future. One baby may start to crawl early, but then still be shuffling along the floor long after her contemporaries have taken their first steps. Others may remain pretty immobile for the first 14 months, but spend their time chattering non-stop instead. Try not to compare your baby to those of your friends (though that can be hard in the cut throat world of first-time parenthood) and let her develop at her own pace. You may find that your baby chooses to ignore some of those supposedly important milestones (such as crawling) and go straight to the next stage instead.

It is worth keeping a diary of your baby's development and any significant 'firsts' – primarily out of interest for yourselves. It is amazing how quickly you forget when these momentous occasions occurred and in years to come it makes interesting reading. It is also useful to have such a diary to take to the development checks your baby will have over the first couple of years, as you are likely to be asked questions such as 'When did she start to pull herself up?', 'When did she start to crawl/walk?' and so on. This is not to test how clever or advanced your baby is, but just to make sure that she is achieving certain milestones within a normal period of time and that there is nothing to be concerned about.

All of the milestones given below are for the 'average baby' (of which there are very few) and a perfectly normal baby may achieve them far earlier or later than these dates – as is proved by babies George and Isaac (see below) whose first years were charted to see how they compared to the 'average baby'.

ALLOWING FOR EARLY ARRIVAL

If you had a premature baby then remember to take that into account for the first two years. For instance, if your baby was born eight weeks prematurely, six months ago, then she may only be reaching the milestones of a four-month-old baby. Baby Isaac, whose progress is charted in the following pages, was only four weeks premature which usually makes a less significant difference. Indeed most babies who are only a few weeks premature tend to catch up over the first year.

MONTH BY MONTH

In this chapter we follow the progress of two babies – George and Isaac – over their first year, as charted by their mothers in a diary. In the lists of recognized milestones, the following aspects of development are considered:

✿ Gross motor skills, meaning physical skills, such as crawling, walking, etc.
✿ Fine motor skills, such as the use of the hands, coordination
✿ Hearing and speech
✿ Social and play skills.

THE NEWBORN BABY

When your baby is born she will:

✿ have a floppy head
✿ have lots of primitive reflexes, such as the stepping reflex
✿ have closed hands
✿ grasp anything put in her hand
✿ startle at any loud sound
✿ briefly focus on your face as it moves across her line of vision
✿ have no other interaction skills.

George

Baby George was a week late and was delivered by an independent midwife in water, weighing 4kg (9lb 2oz). Everything went really well and his mother didn't even have any stitches. They both went home the next day.

Isaac

Baby Isaac was induced four weeks prematurely and was delivered by ventouse, weighing 2.6kg (5lb 10oz). He was in special care for a few days.

THE FIRST MONTH

By the end of this month your baby will probably be able to:

- ✿ lift her head up momentarily when laid on a flat surface
- ✿ focus on your face and start to subtly copy some facial expressions
- ✿ possibly smile at you when you talk to her
- ✿ respond to a noise, such as a bell, by quietening.

George

Motor skills George has changed so much over the first few weeks. He looks less like a wrinkly newborn, his body is less curled up and his eyes have opened up so much more.

Social, play and hearing He is definitely aware of me and my voice and seems very content. I am pretty sure that he has smiled at me already, at about four weeks old. He loves his bath – he's definitely a water baby!

Isaac

Motor skills Isaac has been difficult to feed, but I'm persevering with the breastfeeding. He loves to have a good stretch and extends his arms and legs as far as he can and makes lots of grunting noises. He is so long, perhaps he didn't like being curled up inside me.

Social, play and hearing He loves being close to us and lies in our bed very contentedly. He isn't so keen on being undressed though and doesn't like having a bath at all. When I talk to him in a low soothing voice it seems to quieten him.

THE SECOND MONTH

By the end of this month your baby will probably be able to:

✿ be lifted to a sitting position from a lying position with the head falling back slightly, but not completely

✿ follow an object held 90cm (3ft) away over an angle of 90 degrees

✿ keep her head momentarily in the same plane as the rest of her body when held horizontally, on her front

✿ lift her head 45 degrees when laid on her stomach

✿ smile when spoken to, if you smile at her

✿ follow you with her eyes when you move around the room.

George

Motor skills George has such strong neck control. If I pick him up to a sitting position, he can keep his head in line with his body.

Social, play, vision and hearing If I move a finger slowly from in front of his nose to the left or right of his face about 15cm (6in) away from his face, he follows it with his eyes – and he does seem to watch me as I move around. George is definitely smiling at me now and is making plenty of little chatty noises too.

Isaac

Motor skills He is starting to hold his head up more now (at about six weeks) and when he's in his Moses basket he turns his head to look both ways.

Social, play and hearing He gets excited when I talk to him and is already showing signs of liking music – even my singing! He made his first proper smile at about seven weeks which was lovely and now he smiles whenever he goes off to sleep.

THE THIRD MONTH

By the end of this month your baby will probably be able to:

- ❀ lift her head anything from 45 to 90 degrees when she's laid on her tummy
- ❀ keep her head nearly in line with her body when pulled to a sitting position
- ❀ hold her hands loosely open, having lost the tightly curled hands of a newborn
- ❀ hold a rattle when it is placed in her hand and wave it aimlessly
- ❀ follow an object with her eyes for 180 degrees when it is moved in an arc in front of her face.

She will probably also:

- ❀ vocalize when spoken to
- ❀ turn her head in the direction of a sound
- ❀ be fascinated by her hands and fingers and stare at them intently, bringing them to a midline in front of her eyes.

George

Motor skills George's hand will close around a rattle, but he doesn't really seem aware that he's holding it or when he drops it. I can pull him up to sitting now quite comfortably and we make a little game out of it. He's so active. He'll never sit in a chair for long and will not lie back in my arms.

Social, play, vision and hearing He keeps getting distracted by noises and things going on in the room and will turn his head to have a look when I'm breastfeeding him – nosy boy! He chuckles sometimes.

Isaac

Motor skills He's got very steady neck control now and will lift his head up if I put him flat on his belly, but he doesn't like it much! He'll lie in his Moses basket for long periods of time quite contentedly. He sucks his hands a lot and brings them deliberately to his mouth.

Social, play, vision and hearing He has started to notice himself in a mirror now and smiles at himself. His grins are getting broader and broader and he's making a lot more cooing and gurgling noises.

THE FOURTH MONTH

By the end of this month your baby will probably be able to:

✿ lift her head 90 degrees when she's laid on her tummy

✿ bring her hands together

✿ pull her dress over her face

✿ laugh aloud.

George

Motor skills He rolled over onto his side this week! My mum was so surprised. He seems so full of muscle and energy. When I put him back he did it again. I put him under a baby gym and he'll reach out for the objects and hit them now – I think he's discovered he has got hands!

Social, play and hearing He loves nursery rhymes now and will giggle away when we do 'Round and round the garden'. He seems to anticipate the tickling already.

Isaac

Motor skills He isn't so happy to lie down all the time now – he wants to be up and seeing what's going on. He has now discovered he has two hands! Until now he always showed a preference for the left one.

Social, play and hearing He likes having noises repeated back to him and enjoys the games we play when we change his nappy. (He doesn't mind being undressed now.) He especially likes 'Round and round the garden' and anticipates the tickling.

THE FIFTH MONTH

By the end of this month your baby will probably be able to:

- ✿ lift herself up onto her forearms when put onto her tummy
- ✿ keep her head in line with her body when she is pulled to a sitting position without her head lagging backwards at all
- ✿ roll over one way – usually front to back
- ✿ put her toes in her mouth and play with her toes
- ✿ reach for a toy and grab it
- ✿ pay attention to a very small object, such as a raisin
- ✿ smile spontaneously.

George

Motor and play skills I can sit him up by himself now although I put a pile of cushions behind him to catch him if he falls because he is still rather wobbly. He loves being upright and will reach for a toy to play with by himself. I can also pull him up to a standing position from sitting and hold him standing for a while – his legs seem so strong! He just laughs and looks really proud of himself.

Social skills He is developing attachments to the major people in his life and shows signs of recognizing his grandma and his nanny by giving them both big smiles. He's got his bottom two teeth.

Isaac

Motor skills Isaac isn't sitting up by himself but enjoys sitting with me to see what is happening.

Social and play skills He's become very attached to his muslin square. Socially I can see so many changes – he likes playing peek-a-boo and smiles whenever he sees particular toys, especially Humpty and Little Ted. No teeth yet!

THE SIXTH MONTH

By the end of this month your baby will probably be able to:

- ✿ lift up her chest and take her weight on her hands, with extended arms, when put on her tummy
- ✿ sit on the floor by herself, with her hands on the floor for some support
- ✿ take her full weight on her legs and stand, held
- ✿ roll completely over from front to back, and back again
- ✿ transfer a toy from one hand to the other
- ✿ begin to imitate you coughing or making a noise
- ✿ chew her own food if it is soft.

George

Motor skills George rolls over completely now and is such a wriggler when it comes to changing time. He seems to roll over every time – just because he can! He now can get himself into a sitting position from being on his stomach, but he often gets a leg stuck underneath him. He keeps getting onto all fours and then lifting his legs up so that he's on tiptoe. It looks like he wants to combine walking and crawling, but he doesn't get anywhere! Usually he just trips over a leg and falls over. He likes having teeth and tucks into breadsticks happily. He puts anything he finds into his mouth for a good chew.

Social skills He has started putting his arms up to be picked up – how can I resist?!

Isaac

Motor and play skills Isaac is really enjoying his activity arch now. He lies under it and kicks the toys that hang down. He's very interested in his feet. He is starting to sit up and pulls himself forward in his pushchair or when he's in his bouncy seat, but I can't leave him to sit up on the floor yet. He is still showing no sign of wanting to roll either!

Social, play and hearing skills Isaac doesn't seem very happy in social situations and gets frightened if other babies cry or shout. With me he is very happy and confident though and we play lots of games together. He likes striking out at our piano keys!

THE SEVENTH MONTH

By the end of this month your baby will probably be able to:

- ✿ sit on the floor with no support for a few seconds
- ✿ roll over completely from her back to her tummy
- ✿ bounce, by bending her knees, when you hold her standing
- ✿ feed herself a biscuit
- ✿ attract attention by babbling or some other method
- ✿ turn her head in the direction of a sound below her ear
- ✿ make a wet raspberry blowing sound
- ✿ make two syllable sounds, such as 'Mama', 'Dada', but not with any meaning.

George

Motor skills George has mastered crawling! After tripping up on his legs a few times, he's off! He can also get himself back into a sitting position from a crawling one and get from a sitting position to a standing one by pulling himself up on the furniture – or my legs. When he's up there he shuffles along the furniture if he sees something he fancies at the other end.

Social and play skills He loves playing with his toys now and especially likes banging things and listening to the noise they make.

Isaac

Motor skills He is finally sitting up quite well, but I put lots of cushions behind him still in case he topples backwards. He still won't roll over when I put him on his back and he doesn't like being put on his front at all. I'm still breastfeeding him, but he has started to hold a beaker when I give him some juice and he'll try to drink it by himself, but not very successfully. He reaches out for the toys around him now and everything goes in his mouth.

Social skills I've noticed that he really responds to my voice now and gets very animated.

THE EIGHTH MONTH

By the end of this month your baby will probably be able to:

❀ sit unsupported and lean forward to reach objects
❀ rake for a small object with her hand and pick it up in her fist
❀ look for a dropped object – showing the beginnings of memory
❀ turn her head in the direction of a sound above her ear.

George

Motor skills George's crawling is very proficient. He'll also stand alone now for about 30 seconds, then drop heavily on his bottom! He's happy to sit and play by himself for longer now and is very interested in his toys and everything around him.

Social and play skills He especially likes music and will sit and 'dance' on his bottom! He's much more verbal too and talks in a sing-song way with 'da da' and 'mum-mum'. He's also got a couple of party tricks – he waves bye-bye and if you say 'kisses' will blow you a kiss!

Poor boy – his four top teeth all came through at once this month. There are still only two on the bottom.

Isaac

Motor skills Isaac can sit without cushions now and will pick up toys and pass them from one hand to the other. He chews everything he gets hold of, but there are still no teeth coming through!

Social and play skills He is interested in everything around him and looks out for the squirrels, dogs and ducks in the park. He's beginning to show his own mind too and often arches his back in protest if he doesn't want to go into the pushchair or car seat.

THE NINTH MONTH

By the end of this month your baby will probably be able to:

- ✿ stand holding onto something
- ✿ pull herself to a standing or sitting position
- ✿ crawl on her tummy
- ✿ make an attempt to pick up a small object such as a raisin using her thumb and the tip of her forefinger (between now and the end of the tenth month)
- ✿ poke at objects with her index finger.

She will probably also:

- ✿ start to show a preference for being close to mum and to be fearful of strangers
- ✿ be very interested in what is happening around her.

George

Motor skills Having started standing longer and longer by himself, George has been taking some wobbly steps! He'll stand holding onto something then decide to go to something else without getting down to crawl. I've noticed that he's stopped raking for dropped pieces of food on his highchair and is trying to pick them up with his finger and thumb now.

Social and play skills He thinks it's really funny to drop toys and let you pick them up and he really laughs at anything unusual, such as when I balance a toy on my head. The third bottom tooth has come through.

Isaac

Motor skills Isaac can take all of his weight on his feet now, but he can't pull himself up. I wonder if he'll miss out crawling completely and go straight to walking – he's showing no signs of rolling still. When I give him two blocks to hold he bangs them together and enjoys the sound that makes.

Social and play skills He has started to copy me and will mimic something I do. We play peek-a-boo and he covers up his own face! He will concentrate on one activity for much longer. Socially he seems much more relaxed and he likes other children now.

THE TENTH MONTH

By the end of this month your baby will probably be able to:

- ✿ crawl on her hands and knees, with her tummy lifted
- ✿ switch from sitting to lying and back again.
- ✿ pull herself to a sitting position
- ✿ wave bye-bye
- ✿ play pat-a-cake and peek-a-boo
- ✿ help you dress her by holding out an arm for a coat or a foot for a shoe. She will also transfer anything she's holding into the other hand so that you can put a sleeve on.

She will probably also:

- ✿ object if you take a toy away
- ✿ say 'Mama' or 'Dada' indiscriminately.

George

Motor skills George is walking around quite happily, although he'll sometimes drop to his crawling position. He also drinks from his beaker by himself now which is easier than bottlefeeding for me.

Social and play skills He's such a little character and interacts with you so much more, you have no doubt about what he wants. He'll point at the biscuit tin when it comes out and complain loudly if you take away something that he was playing with – however dangerous it is! He realizes when I'm saying 'No' to him, and often responds to it, but sometimes he'll just laugh at me! His fourth bottom tooth is through.

Isaac

Motor skills Isaac will spin around 180 degrees while he's lying on his back in his cot, but he still won't roll onto his tummy and, although he will rotate on his bottom to reach for a toy, he still won't crawl to get something! He does like to stand with me holding him though so perhaps walking is more likely.

Social and play skills Spending all this time on his bottom has helped his concentration, and he'll sit and turn the pages of a board book for ages. He's copying the silly animal noises I make now, such as a pig's snort and a duck's quack. His first tooth has finally appeared!

THE ELEVENTH MONTH

By the end of this month your baby will probably be able to:

- ✿ offer something to you, but not necessarily release it
- ✿ say one word with meaning, possibly 'Dada' for daddy
- ✿ pivot around while sitting on the floor without overbalancing
- ✿ walk by holding onto the furniture
- ✿ walk if you hold both her hands
- ✿ understand the word 'No', but not necessarily obey it.

George

Motor and play skills He loves balls and will chase them around the house for as long as we'll play with him – sometimes he'll even roll it back to me when I've rolled it towards him. His other favourite game is putting his wooden blocks into a saucepan.

Social skills George is saying 'Dada', but seems to use it for both me and his dad! He knows his own name well now and will always turn when we call him. He also seems to have developed his own little language. He babbles away in it as if he's talking, but it certainly isn't English!

Isaac

Motor skills He is standing holding onto the furniture now and getting quite frustrated I think because he wants to walk and can't. He enjoys going around with his baby walker instead. He can pick up small pieces of food with his finger and thumb now and tries to feed me!

Social skills He is showing a lot more understanding of the world and will point at things, such as a duck, dad, clock and pig, when asked. When I ask him where his toes are, he takes off his socks and points to them! He definitely knows his own name and will turn when called – he likes waving to himself in a mirror too!

THE TWELFTH MONTH

By the end of this month your baby will probably be able to:

- ✿ say two or three words with meaning
- ✿ walk on her hands and feet like a bear
- ✿ walk upright with one hand held
- ✿ throw objects, one after another
- ✿ hand a toy over to her mother.

George

Motor skills He is getting so noisy and boisterous, sometimes I wish he hadn't started walking so early. He now loves emptying his basket of toys systematically and often just chucking them over his shoulder without even looking at them! When the box is empty he just wanders off, while I end up tidying after him. I can't leave him alone for a minute. Even if I turn my back on him when he's in his pushchair, he'll try to climb out of the harness – and he often protests at being put in by making himself completely rigid. What will he be like when he's two?

Social skills I think George has said 'Mama' now, referring to me, but it could be wishful thinking!

Isaac

Motor skills I've noticed that Isaac sometimes rolls onto his belly when he's asleep now – about time! He still hasn't crawled, but likes walking around holding onto my hand instead. It looks as if I'll never see him on all fours! He is opening and shutting the cupboards now and enjoys emptying any boxes he comes across. He is far more dextrous and can fit interlocking pieces together and post objects through the holes. He will even feed himself from a spoon, but it's so messy!

Social skills He is pointing like mad at anything he wants and if he doesn't get it he shouts loudly. I think I'll have my work cut out!

There are certain milestones which are taken seriously, and if your baby has not reached them by the age suggested below, then you should mention it to your health visitor or doctor. You should do this if your baby:

- ✿ has an uncertain response to sounds
- ✿ is not following a face by six weeks
- ✿ still has a squint at six months
- ✿ is not sitting by 7–8 months
- ✿ is not walking by 18 months.

However, do not spend hours analysing every move your baby makes in fear that you might overlook the fact that she has not reached a particular milestone at the appropriate time. Stories abound of children who did not utter a single word until they were two years old and then started talking in complete sentences almost immediately. Other children choose not to walk until they have had their second birthday, finding their bottoms or knees a far better means of getting about. Often these 'unusual' children will develop quite quickly in other areas instead. For instance, the late walker may have a more advanced vocabulary and the late talker may be far more adept at climbing and ball skills.

Every baby is unique and has her own rate of progress. Most babies achieve everything in their own time.

I got so fed up with the apparent competition between mothers of babies the same age as my Jack. I was always having to listen to comments such as 'How many teeth has he got now? Still only one, oh dear...'. I understand that new mums need reassurance that their baby is normal, but sometimes the remarks got quite rude. Eventually I distanced myself from the postnatal coffee mornings and mixed with parents of children of different ages – it was far more relaxing!

Maxine, mother to Jack, nine months old.

DISCIPLINE – DOES YOUR BABY NEED IT?

Discipline sounds rather a harsh word
to use in the context of a baby's first year,
but the word is more appropriate when
taken back to its original form, which is the
Latin word, *disciplina*, meaning 'teaching'.

As parents you are there to teach your
baby the ways of the world and to show her, through word and
example, how she may grow up happy, sociable and able. This does not
mean constantly shouting at her when she does something you believe
to be wrong, but giving her plenty of love and attention, and allowing
her to gradually learn from you what is dangerous or socially
unacceptable. A baby does not do something 'naughty' on purpose. It's
like the reason for climbing Everest – she pulls the tablecloth because it
is there, and wants to play with your precious jewellery because it
sparkles. She does not understand the implications of what she is doing
and will not for some time.

Setting rules and guidelines at an early age (around ten months or
so) will also help your baby feel more secure. A child actually likes to
have limits to work within – even if they spend most of their time
testing them at a later date – so start instilling good routines and habits
as soon as she becomes aware of herself as an individual.

HOW TO TEACH HER

Start to say 'No' Once your baby becomes mobile she becomes a
danger to herself – and, less importantly, your belongings. This is
the time to start saying 'No', softly but firmly, and removing her or
the article in question. Eventually she'll come to recognize the word
(at around nine months), but she may not necessarily act on it. In
fact it's more than likely that she'll stop, look at you, laugh and go
back to doing exactly the same thing once again! That doesn't
matter. Just stick to your guns and continue to say 'No' in the same
firm but gentle voice. Babies have very short memories, but
eventually, sometime after her first birthday, she'll begin to get the
idea – then she'll spend the whole of the second year defying you!

*Everyone talks about the special relationship that twins
have, but my two don't seem to have that. They play
alongside each other rather than together and now and then
they bite each other. Is there something I'm doing wrong?*

Sue, mother to Imogen and Molly, 12 months old.

Twins usually do have a good relationship but at 12
months they are too young to realize this yet. By two and
a half years old children watch siblings/other children
with interest and may occasionally join in a game for a
few minutes, but little notion of sharing goes on until
around three years old, when playing together becomes
more obvious.

Praise the good   It is just as important to praise your baby's good
behaviour so that she understands which of her actions are
welcomed by you and will get a good response whenever she
repeats them. So don't hold back on the congratulations when she
tries to say 'Ta' or responds to a warning from you, and quietly point
out the error of her ways when she does something less acceptable.
Congratulations and rewards are far more effective than
punishments.

Be united   There is little point in one parent being firm about
something when the other lets her get away with it. As parents
you have got to be united on what you expect from your children
and how you make that clear. Your baby will never learn if she is
getting confusing signals all the time. She wants to know where
she stands.

Set her a good example   Forget the old saying 'Don't do as I do, do
as I say' and remember that your baby will learn from watching how
you behave, towards her and to others.

We've moved everything we care about out of reach so we don't have
to keep saying 'No' to Tom in order to protect our treasures — only if
he's going for something dangerous that might hurt him, or if he's
going to hurt another child by being rough. I think this has worked
because I don't have to say 'No' to him all the time and when I do say
it he listens and knows I mean it.

Suzie, mother to Tom, 11 months old.

Remember that all babies are different   What works for one parent might not work for you. You will discover how your baby ticks and what is the best way of teaching her good habits and reminding her which are not so good.

The most important lesson is love   When your baby feels happy and confident that you love her, she will learn from you and your example all the more readily.

6

Your baby's health

When you first become a parent, everything is so strange and new that it is hard to tell what is normal and what might be a sign of something

more worrying. For the first few months you peer into dirty nappies, listen anxiously to his cry, fret over every pimple and rush him off to the doctor at the slightest cough. Then you gradually begin to relax and gain some confidence in your abilities and instincts. You get to know your child and are able to tell as soon as he is slightly off colour – and when he might need medical attention. Go with those instincts – you are his mother and you know him better than any health professional.

Whenever you suspect there is a problem, listen to and act on what the doctor has to say, but if you think it necessary, ask for a second opinion. A mother's instincts are often right.

A TO Z OF COMMON AILMENTS

This chapter is designed to help you put your mind at rest over what may be nothing to worry about and give you some tips for treating minor common ailments at home. It will also, it is hoped, make you aware of the signs of anything more serious so that you can take the appropriate action quickly. It does not in any way claim to be a substitute for proper medical attention. When in doubt, make an appointment to see your doctor.

ASTHMA

The signs   Recurrent, but intermittent attacks of breathlessness with wheezing are the classic signs, but it can range from a mild breathlessness to significant difficulty in breathing. Your baby may produce more phlegm than normal and develop a dry cough, often at night. It can develop at any age, but most sufferers have their first attack before they are five.

What it is   The small airways in the lungs are caused to narrow by any of a number of things (including a cold, or allergens such as pollen, housedust, milk, cats and dogs), making it hard for your baby to breathe – and the cough is his way of trying to clear the airways. Sometimes the cause is intrinsic though, meaning there is no apparent external cause for the asthma.

What to do   Consult your doctor. There is no cure for asthma, but attacks can be prevented. Skin testing can sometimes identify allergens and then you can help to avoid your child coming into contact with them by damp dusting (to reduce dustmites), removing offending pets, feather pillows and duvets and so on. Your baby will usually be prescribed a drug to relax and widen the airways when inhaled. He may also be given inhaled steroids which are usually effective in reducing the number of attacks in babies who suffer frequently.

CHEST INFECTION

The signs   A chest infection can start life as a simple cold, but your baby becomes feverish and has a fruity, productive cough sometimes accompanied by a wheezy chest. Your baby may seem very unwell with it, but some cope quite well during the day and are only bothered at night (making it particularly bothersome for you parents!).

What it is   Chest infections can occur as a result of either a viral or a bacterial infection. Small babies are particularly vulnerable to a viral infection known as bronchiolitis, caused by the respiratory syncytial virus (RSV), which crops up in seasonal epidemics in winter. Bacterial infections are less common although babies with asthma or those born prematurely are more at risk.

What to do   Sometimes your baby will get a cough that doesn't seem to bother him too much and you can soldier on together. At other times though, it may bother him to the extent that you think some medical help may be necessary. If it is a bacterial infection, treatment with antibiotics usually brings about a prompt improvement.

CHICKENPOX

The signs   This common disease varies in severity from child to child. For small babies (under a month old) it can be very serious, but for an older baby it is usually only a very mild illness. The spots or rash start as small, itchy, red spots, but turn to fluid-filled blisters about 2–3mm (1/8in) in diameter within a few hours. Sometimes the rash is accompanied by a slightly raised temperature.

What it is   Chickenpox is caused by the varicella-zoster virus, but that makes it sound far worse than it is. The virus is spread in the air and children are most infectious from about two days before the rash appears until about a week later when the scabs have healed. For most children it is just a mild inconvenience (albeit not a very attractive one).

What to do   If your newborn catches it or is exposed to it consult your doctor immediately as it may be prudent to give him an anti-viral drug treatment. For the older baby, however, no drugs or treatment are necessary – just a bit of rest. Infant paracetamol can be given to reduce any fever and your baby should be feeling better within ten days. Try to stay out of circulation until then, and keep your baby's nails short so that he can't scratch the blisters and infect them.

> When Lucy developed chickenpox I dressed her in long sleeves and trousers the whole time, and cut her nails really short so that she couldn't scratch the spots. She did pick one on her chin, but it didn't leave a scar, luckily.
>
> Rebecca, mother to Lucy, one year old.

COMMON COLD

The signs   Well, you know what it feels like yourself – a blocked or snuffly nose, a raised temperature, a bad night's sleep and a lack of appetite. It's not surprising that babies get grumpy when they have a cold – especially as they are used to being able to breathe through their noses while they feed.

What it is   The common cold is caused by a virus – of which there are always plenty of different types about. You cannot catch one simply because you get cold or wet and the bad news is that you can easily become infected by the same virus again.

What to do   If your baby has a raised temperature then give him infant paracetamol at regular intervals to bring it down and if he's not feeding well, offer a bottlefed baby some water now and then. Do not overwrap him to keep him warm – you do not want him to overheat.

There is little point in taking your baby to a doctor unless you think the cold may have developed into a chest or ear infection (or your baby is unable to feed because of his blocked-up nose). The doctor can't do anything to cure a common cold and can only offer commonsense advice to reduce the symptoms.

CONSTIPATION

The signs   Pretty obvious! Nothing happening down below.
What it is If your baby does not get enough to drink (plenty of watery foremilk if you are breastfeeding or bottles of cooled, boiled water, if you are bottlefeeding), then his stools will become firm and harder to pass. If your baby is on solids, he needs plenty of fibre (found in fruit, vegetables, bread and cereal) in order to make regular bowel movements.
What to do   A baby doesn't make regular bowel movements like an adult – some babies may only produce something twice a week – so don't get too wound up about the non-appearance of anything solid each day. If your baby seems well and is eating and drinking well, then you have nothing to worry about. If, however, it continues and your baby seems miserable, or if there is any bleeding because the stools are hard to pass then go and see your doctor. She may prescribe a mild laxative to soften the stool, or may just suggest giving your baby some diluted fruit juice.

CRADLE CAP

The signs   Thick yellow scales which cannot easily be brushed away appear on your baby's scalp (and sometimes also on the face, neck, behind the ears and in the nappy area). It can sometimes look inflamed and red and it tends to recur.

What it is Cradle cap is a temporary skin condition designed to upset all new mothers who want their baby to look as beautiful as possible at all times. The official line is that it's a form of seborrhoeic dermatitis.

What to do There is no need to seek medical attention, unless it seems to be getting worse or the skin becomes inflamed, in which case the doctor may prescribe an ointment. Try rubbing olive oil into your baby's scalp and leave it on overnight to loosen the scales. Rinse it off the next morning, rubbing gently to wash away the scales. You may need to do this for several days to get rid of them all. Brushing your baby's hair with a soft brush will also help to dislodge the scales. There are some specially designed shampoos for treating cradle cap available over the counter from a pharmacy.

> I found that the cradle cap itself didn't bother Rosie, but because it looked unsightly — she didn't have much hair at the time — I bought lots of little hats for her to wear when I took her out!
>
> Karen, mother to Roseanna, 11 months old.

DIARRHOEA

The signs Again, not too hard to miss. You have just become accustomed to the amazing things your baby can fill his nappy with then he presents you with something even more watery, runny and pongy than ever before.

What it is Your baby can develop diarrhoea or be sick for a number of reasons, most of them not at all sinister. If he just presents you with a few nasty nappies, then it may be that he's teething or some fruit juice or a certain solid has disagreed with him. Sometimes it happens for no apparent reason at all. Sometimes the upset tummy is due to an infection, but not necessarily a gut one. It could be the result of an ear infection or a cold.

What to do   More important than the cause of the runny bottom, or the diarrhoea itself, is your treatment of it. As with frequent vomiting, you must not let your baby become dehydrated (the signs of which are a dry mouth and sunken eyes and fontanelle), so make sure he has plenty of fluids – these are more important than calories at the moment. In fact the diarrhoea will clear up more quickly if you can stop giving your baby any solid food at all and, if your baby is bottlefed, replace the milk feeds with water or a commercial rehydration solution for half a day or so. If you are breastfeeding then continue to feed your baby, but feed him more frequently so that he is getting plenty of watery foremilk. If your baby continues to vomit or becomes listless, see your doctor.

When your baby appears to be on the mend, reintroduce the solids and formula feeds very gradually; it is best to dilute formula to half strength for the first day.

Teddy has diarrhoea so often I'm beginning to feel like a bit of an expert! The first couple of times I worried about him being hungry and couldn't bring myself to cut out the formula and solids, but I found the diarrhoea always lingered then. As soon as I was tough and just gave him fluids other than milk for 12 hours it seemed to do the trick.

Claudia, mother to Teddy, nine months old.

EAR INFECTION (OTITIS MEDIA)

The signs   Severe earache and a raised temperature, making your baby miserable. Sometimes the cheeks become flushed and your baby gives you an extra clue by tugging at his ears.

What it is   The pain is caused by inflammation of the middle ear – the result of a viral or bacterial infection (such as a common cold). Sometimes the eardrum bursts, which relieves the pain and results in a discharge from the ear. Frequent ear infections can sometimes lead to a continual production of sticky fluid in the middle ear – a condition referred to as 'glue ear'. About one in six children suffer from ear infections in their first year.

What to do   Take your baby to have his ears checked by a doctor as soon as possible if you suspect that he may have an ear infection. The doctor will probably prescribe antibiotics, although it may be that the infection is caused by a virus and the antibiotics (which help to fight bacteria) will have little effect. In the meantime, give him infant paracetamol to bring down any fever and reduce the pain.

> Charlie does seem very prone to ear infections. Every time he has a cold it develops into one. It is so miserable, before I take him to the doctors we tend to have one night of screaming when nothing seems to settle him, but the antibiotics do take effect very quickly – in a matter of hours. The doctor says that Charlie as an individual will not become resistant to the antibiotics – it is the nation as a whole that runs the risk of becoming so if we overuse them.
>
> Cathy, mother to Charlie, one year old.

ECZEMA

The signs   Areas of your baby's skin (especially the hands, back of the knees, the face and the inner crease of the elbows) become covered in a dry, itchy rash. The skin sometimes forms scales and small red pimples can appear which ooze when they are scratched. The areas can become infected if scratched or if the rash is in the nappy area.

What it is   Atopic eczema (as described above) is common in babies between the ages of 2 and 18 months – especially if there is a history of allergies in the family. It can be caused by an allergy, or it can flare up for no apparent reason. The good news is that babies often grow out of it. Similar skin inflammations are sometimes referred to as dermatitis.

What to do   If the eczema isn't too bad, and your baby isn't bothered by it, then start treatment at home by covering the affected areas frequently in an emollient such as aqueous cream or petroleum jelly to keep it moist and prevent it from cracking. Also try dressing your baby only in cotton, avoiding soap and nappy wipes and switching to a milder form of detergent for washing his clothes. If that doesn't seem to work then show the problem areas to your doctor. She may prescribe corticosteroid drugs if it is severe.

> When Tom was born, and for the first eight months, he was very prone to getting patches of eczema on his cheeks, behind his ears and under his chin. I have eczema myself so I was really anxious about it, but by keeping it soft with aqueous cream and not dressing him in woolies we seem to have beaten it. He has not had any for the past three months.
>
> Martyn, father to Tom, one year old.

HEAT RASH (RED SPOTS)

The signs   Small, flat, red spots, which sometimes join into larger patches. They are commonly seen on the cheeks (especially if you are breastfeeding) of a newborn, but they can also appear in areas where clothes are tight, the creases of the neck and your baby's middle. They sometimes develop small, hard, yellow pustules in the middle.

What it is   No one really knows what causes these spots, though heat is usually blamed and babies who are breastfeeding can get quite

warm when they are stuck under your jumper for a large part of the
day. Sometimes babies develop a rash as a result of a viral infection so
don't always assume that a rash is just a result of overheating.

What to do If your baby is happy and well, then don't worry about
heat rash, it will disappear quite quickly. If, however, your baby seems
to show any other unusual signs, such as a raised temperature, then
consult your doctor. (Also see Meningitis, below.)

INFANT SPOTS (MILIA)

The signs Little yellow spots, mostly around the bridge of the nose on
a newborn.

What it is This is a condition that usually appears in the first few days
due to the immature skin glands springing into action.

What to do Absolutely nothing. Definitely don't squeeze them or
treat them as you might a teenage spot. They will disappear of their
own accord in a week or so.

MENINGITIS

The signs To start with, the symptoms can be similar to those of flu.
In babies look out for signs of a fever (yet the hands and feet are cold); a
loss of appetite or vomiting; a high-pitched moaning cry or whimper; a
blank expression; a loss of energy; a pale and blotchy complexion; and a
dislike of bright lights. He may also lie with his head extended. The signs
may not all appear at once – some take one or two days to develop or
they can appear in just a few hours. Sometimes the meningitis bacteria
causes blood poisoning (septicaemia) and, as a result, a rash develops
which will not turn white when pressed under a glass.

What it is There are two types of meningitis – viral and bacterial. Both
result in inflammation of the lining of the brain, but viral meningitis is

hardly ever life threatening, whereas bacterial meningitis can lead to permanent deafness, brain damage or death if not treated quickly.
What to do If you suspect meningitis, phone your doctor immediately or, if you cannot get a response there, go straight to your nearest hospital emergency department. If your baby has bacterial meningitis he will need antibiotics as soon as possible. Viral meningitis cannot be treated by antibiotics and your baby will just need plenty of good nursing care.

NAPPY RASH

The signs Your baby's skin will look pink and inflamed in the nappy area and, if allowed to get worse, can become broken.
What it is Your baby has sensitive skin which is easily irritated by substances in his urine and faeces and becomes inflamed. Most commonly it tends to occur if your baby is filling his nappy frequently or is left for too long in a dirty or wet nappy.
What to do If your baby already has nappy rash then treat it with a medicated nappy cream and leave his bottom bare for long periods to let it 'air'. If it does not seem to improve and becomes worse, then see your doctor who may prescribe a corticosteroid and an antifungal cream. Prevention is better than cure however, so change your baby's nappy frequently (after every feed) and use a barrier cream to protect your baby's bottom if you use towelling nappies which do not absorb the wetness so well as disposables.

ORAL THRUSH

The signs Little white patches on the cheeks inside your baby's mouth, and on his tongue. Many people think these are just milk residues, but if you try to remove them you'll find they stay put and may even bleed.

What it is   Quite common after a course of treatment with antibiotics, oral thrush is an infection caused by a fungus called *Candida albicans*. Don't immediately start blaming yourself for a lack of cleanliness though, your baby could have caught it during delivery or from anything he has put in his mouth, as keeping everything totally sterile is impossible. Many babies are totally oblivious to the fact that they are causing their parents any concern, but occasionally it can be painful and interfere with their feeding.

What to do   Most doctors will prescribe an antifungal treatment in the form of a liquid which you apply to the tongue.

SICKY BABY (GASTRO-OESOPHAGEAL REFLUX)

The signs   It seems that your baby brings up nearly as much milk as he's taken down! Whenever you pick him up you get a charming milky deposit on your shoulder and your washing machine is on the go the whole time. Some babies are affected so badly that it prevents them from gaining adequate weight.

What it is   The valve at the top of a baby's stomach which helps to keep the food down is very immature and needs time to become 100 per cent effective. For some babies it is particularly unreliable and a lot of what is taken down manages to escape and make a reappearance.

What to do   First, buy plenty of bibs. If your baby is happy and gaining weight adequately then you'll just have to sling a muslin square permanently over your shoulder, grin and bear it. If however, it seems that your baby is not putting on enough weight or there are traces of blood in the milk (due to the stomach acid upsetting the oesophagus), then you should talk to your doctor about the problem. He may suggest using a medicine to help the milk move in the right direction and prescribe a special milk thickener. Usually though, babies just grow out of it naturally once they start to sit up by themselves, and moving onto solids helps.

Emma Lydia was sicky from the word go. I found having a huge stack of muslin squares helped a lot. We always had one to hand and one draped over our shoulders! Funnily enough, once she began to have solids, she wasn't so sick, but she developed a fondness for her 'cloth' and it has become her comforter. She will not go to sleep without it now and it is quite useful when she's upset.

Fiona, mother to Emma Lydia, ten months old.

STICKY EYE

The signs   The eyes are often stuck together in the mornings with a sticky yellow discharge and throughout the day it will emerge from the corner of the eye. If it develops into an infection, the inside of the eyelids become red and swollen too.

What it is   Many babies suffer from sticky eye in the first few days. For most it remains only a minor irritation, but sometimes it develops into an infection.

What to do   It is worth taking your baby to the doctor so that she can decide whether or not it is an infection and prescribe ointment if necessary. Bathing your baby's eyes with cooled, boiled water will help – using a separate piece of cottonwool for each eye so that you don't transfer the infection.

TEETHING

The signs   Look out for grumpiness, difficulty in sleeping and a lot more dribble than normal. You may not be able to see the tooth that is causing the problem, but might notice a red and swollen area on the gum. According to your grandmother, diarrhoea, vomiting, nappy rash and loss of appetite are also typical signs, but don't ever dismiss any of these symptoms as being 'just teething' as your baby may be suffering from some other disorder.

What it is   This hardly warrants an explanation. Some teeth are coming through and giving your baby grief. Sometimes there will be a huge song and dance about one tooth making its way to the surface, then another will come through almost unnoticed. Usually the bottom two central incisors appear first, followed by the two above. Next come the canines on either side of these, then the first molars (between 13 and 19 months). Basically, your baby could be teething at any time from five months to three years old.

What to do   Give your baby plenty of things to chew on to help alleviate the pain. Anything from teething rings to a piece of firm apple will do, and it is particularly effective if it's chilled. You can also buy teething gel to rub on the affected gum and give your baby infant paracetamol if he seems in pain. Also stock up on the towelling bibs to absorb all that dribble.

WHEN TO SEE THE DOCTOR

You will know instinctively when something is not right, and when it is worth getting proper medical attention, but as a guide, your baby may give you one or more of the clues listed here if he is ill.

See the doctor if your baby:

- ✿ is unusually sleepy and much less active
- ✿ is having breathing difficulties
- ✿ feels hot while looking pale
- ✿ takes less than half of his normal feeds for a day
- ✿ has diarrhoea and no wet nappies.

You should certainly see the doctor immediately if your baby:

- ✿ looks withdrawn, distant and sickly
- ✿ looks frightened, pale and has a cold sweat
- ✿ has rapid or laboured breathing for some time
- ✿ is crying as if in severe pain and cannot be consoled.

If you are in any doubt – see the doctor.

IMMUNIZATION – WHY IT'S IMPORTANT

Years ago babies were at risk from a wide variety of diseases, some of them fatal, but today, thanks to immunizations, these diseases are less prevalent in the industrialized world and your baby can be protected against them. In order for us to keep outbreaks of these diseases to a minimum it is important that everyone takes their baby to be immunized at the appropriate times. When you get the call-up from your doctor's surgery, make sure you keep your appointment. The schedule for immunization varies slightly across the world, but in the UK it is as follows:

Two months old
   1st diphtheria, tetanus, whooping cough, polio and Hib
Three months old
   2nd diphtheria, tetanus, whooping cough, polio and Hib
Four months old
   3rd diphtheria, tetanus, whooping cough, polio and Hib
12–18 months
   Measles, mumps, rubella (MMR)

WHAT ARE THESE ILLNESSES?

Take a look at the possible outcomes of contracting any of these illnesses and you'll agree that immunization is a good idea.
Diphtheria   This is an infection of the throat which can cause a fatal obstruction to your baby's breathing or release poisons into your baby's bloodstream. It can result in paralysis or heart failure.
Tetanus   Commonly known as 'lockjaw', this disease is caused by an organism found in good old everyday dirt. If your baby cuts himself and the organism enters the wound, it can cause spasms and fatal respiratory failure.
Whooping cough   Small babies are most at risk from this illness which causes a spasm of coughing. Your baby cannot catch his breath and so 'whoops' to try and get air back into his lungs. He often ends up vomiting too, which is all very distressing for everyone.
Polio   This disease is caused by a virus and can result in permanent paralysis.

Haemophilus influenzae **type B**   In the past, before the widespread use of the Hib vaccine, this was the most common cause of bacterial meningitis in children (see Meningitis, page 150).

Measles   Everyone knows about the rash, but measles also causes a high fever, bad vomiting, a nasty cough and sore eyes – making babies feel very unhappy indeed. It can even cause encephalitis and pneumonia – both very serious conditions.

Mumps   This is a relatively mild illness compared to those above, resulting in the swelling of the glands below the jaw, but as it can be an uncomfortable illness if caught by an adult male (the testes also become inflamed) it was added to the immunization programme.

Rubella   This is a viral infection also known as German measles. It's not too troublesome for young children but if a pregnant woman catches it it can affect the foetus and cause severe birth defects.

TAKING YOUR BABY TO BE IMMUNIZED

Your baby can be immunized even if he has a cold or is taking a medicine, but check with the nurse first. The only time you should not take your baby to be immunized is if (a) he has or is recovering from a very feverish illness or (b) he has an illness or is taking a medicine that might interfere with his ability to fight infection.

If you don't think you can stand the trauma or guilt of holding out your baby's leg to be injected then you can always ask someone else to hold him while you wait outside, but as he gets older, it's likely that he will want to be with mum.

You will be told of the possible side-effects to look out for, but usually they do not cause any problem. With the first three lots of immunizations some babies become grumpy and feverish after 6–24 hours and they may develop a red mark around the site of the injection. You can give him an infant paracetamol to make him feel more comfortable if necessary.

It takes a week to ten days for the MMR injection to display any side-effects. Your baby may be a bit feverish for one or two days, but that is nothing to worry about. Some children also develop a mild measles rash and a slight swelling around the jaw two or three weeks later.

ALTERNATIVE REMEDIES

These seem to have become increasingly fashionable over recent years as we have become more sceptical abut conventional drugs and worried that we might be overusing them. In a backlash against the advance of modern science a growing number of people are now wondering if historically used natural remedies may be more effective, and have fewer side-effects.

If you start to ask around you will always find someone who claims that they or their baby has been cured by aromatherapy, homeopathy, osteopathy or another form of 'alternative' medicine. So should you risk using 'alternative' methods on your baby? As there are so many strong arguments both for and against this, it really has to come down to personal choice, but consider the following:

- ✿ You don't have to fall into one camp or the other – you could always try the drugs suggested by your doctor then go for something else if they do not seem to work.
- ✿ If you do want to try an alternative therapy consult a properly registered practitioner. Essential oils and homeopathic medicines can be strong and even dangerous if taken ill advisedly – especially if you are treating a baby.
- ✿ Tell your doctor that you are going elsewhere for treatment. In some areas doctors have made links with alternative practitioners and will be able to recommend one to you. Other doctors can be very sceptical of natural therapies, but they may want to register the fact that you are trying it on your baby's notes.

7

Your new life

PARENTS AND LOVERS – YOUR
RELATIONSHIP WITH YOUR PARTNER

There is no doubt about it, becoming a parent will change the
dynamics of your relationship with your partner completely. Once upon
a time you had all the time in the world for each other. There were no
distractions, no interruptions, no responsibilities – except perhaps for
the hours spent at work. You could enjoy long lie-ins, nip out for a drink
when you wanted and head off on holiday at the very last minute. Most
importantly perhaps, everything might have been very democratically

balanced. You probably both went to work, both saw your own set of friends and both enjoyed leaping into bed together for a spot of lustful activity every now and then. Having a baby changes all that, for a while at least.

After your baby is born, the balance of your relationship shifts in a way that our mothers or mother's mothers might have accepted, but which we modern 'having it all' twenty- and thirty-somethings find very hard to swallow. Mother Nature has laid down the rules so that if we are to give our babies the best food available, the mother has to breastfeed – which, in the early weeks, makes it almost impossible for her to leave her baby for anything more than an hour at a time. So, now it is just the male who goes out to work and sees his friends, while the new mother stays at home and looks after the baby.

For many mothers this is fine, but for plenty of others it is hard to adjust to. Understandably, you feel that, although you love your baby very much and do want to be there for her, you would also quite like a taste of the life you used to have and be able to work and play in the way you used to. It is easy to become jealous and resentful of your partner and to find yourself wondering if life and your relationship will ever be the same again.

Meanwhile the new dad is also feeling rather anxious because he now feels under pressure to be a major breadwinner and support this new family. He goes to work (after little sleep too), works harder than before, then comes home at the worst possible time of day to find a grumpy baby and a frazzled partner. Soon he too is wondering what happened to the life they used to have as a couple and whether it will ever be the same again.

Then there's your sex life – another contentious issue. Many new dads and mums can't wait for normal play to resume, but for others it's not so easy. Some new fathers find that being a witness to the birth curbs their desire, leaving them anxious that they will hurt their partner or (worse still?) make her pregnant again! As for the new mothers, breastfeeding not only tends to reduce a woman's libido, it can also dry the vagina. And, while many a woman loves her new curvy figure, there are plenty of others who feel their large milk-filled breasts are not in the slightest bit sexy – and can't believe that their partner still fancies them when their stomach isn't the flat, toned board it used to be. The dads, in their turn, can't understand why their partners are not as keen as they used to be and so feel rejected. Then, of course, there's the sheer exhaustion of breastfeeding and parenthood – not forgetting the fact that if, against all the odds, you do make a dash for the bedroom, you can guarantee that your little angel will decide it's time to wake up and have a good bawl. With this in mind, it is really hard to fathom how some people believe having a baby will bring them closer together!

MOVING FORWARDS

So, what are the answers to this seemingly endless list of complaints? Simplistic as it may seem, time and patience are usually the best healers. The first few months can be shaky, but if you hang in there, you'll soon look back and realize how far you have come. By the time your baby is six months old, she'll be eating solid food, sleeping through the night (hopefully) and you'll be feeding her far less yourself or will have switched to bottles completely. All of this will give you much more energy, a clearer head to reason with and more time to be yourself. With the help of a babysitter you and your partner can (and should) make time to be simply a couple again and rediscover what it was that brought you close enough together to have a baby in the first place.

In the meantime, keep talking to one another about how you feel, and try to laugh at the hiccups in your relationship. If you can't get out as a couple, then make the effort to have some time together in the evenings. Turn the television off and have a quiet dinner, or snuggle up on the sofa. You may not feel like sex, but that doesn't mean you can't make time for cuddles or a relaxing massage. Try to avoid bickering about who does most to look after the baby or to keep the house clean, but talk the problems out instead until you are both happy with the solution. Listen to each other and accept that both of you are finding it hard – so there's little point in scoring points off each other for who is doing the most or having the toughest time. A relationship needs to be worked at all the time, but especially when you become a family. If you can talk things through now and be happy together, despite the stress and lack of sleep, you'll be setting a good example for your children to follow in years to come.

In the past, men expended their physical energy at work, but now they are more likely to be working in an office all day while their partner does a lot of physically tiring work at home with the baby. As a result, men tend to come home tense from lack of exercise and seeking a release through sex, only to find their partner exhausted and not at all interested. Encouraging your partner to have a game of football or squash twice a week will help to relieve his tension and may create more of an equilibrium at home – but it would be even better if you could go out and enjoy an activity together.

Sally, health visitor.

Don't avoid having sex because you think you'll be interrupted by your baby. It's better to have had a go and got only so far, than not to have had any intimacy at all.

Clare, health visitor.

Q

I'm finding intercourse really painful and it has put me off completely. I think my husband wonders if we are ever going to have a sex life again.

Julie, mother to Hugh, nine months old.

There are several reasons why a new mother may find intercourse painful or uncomfortable, but these are the most common:

Feeling tense   If you are worried about sex now that you've had a baby, then you will find it hard to relax and your vagina will be dry, both of which will make intercourse uncomfortable. You could try spending longer on foreplay to help you relax and using a lubricant to ease the dryness.

Stitches   If you have had an episiotomy you may find it hard to relax because you are aware that you have had stitches in this delicate area. However, once the episiotomy has healed there is usually nothing to worry about. Talk to your partner about how you feel and go easy until you feel confident.

Tender scar tissue around the episiotomy site
Occasionally a woman will develop very tender scar tissue around the site of the episiotomy which makes wearing tight jeans and intercourse painful. This can often be treated with oestrogen creams and a lubricant such as KY jelly, but in some cases the scar tissue has to be removed under general anaesthetic. Talk to your doctor if you are worried this is the case.

We have tried to get our sex life going, but it seems that every time we get anywhere Anna wakes up and cries. By the time I've gone in to settle her, I've either gone off the idea or Steve is feeling snubbed because I've put the baby first again. What can I do?

Karen, mother to Anna, seven months old.

Don't feel guilty for going to settle your baby down again. You are biologically driven to put your baby's needs before your partner's – and for good reason. Your baby will not understand if you do not come when she cries, whereas your partner should hopefully be able to see your point of view. The problem is that three can be a crowd – even if it is your family you are referring to – and it will be you who ends up in the middle trying to please everyone, except yourself. Talk to your partner about how you feel, listen to how he feels and in time you should come to some understanding. Also suggest that he goes to settle the baby rather than you, if that would help.

We decided to ask my mother to look after George for the weekend about four times a year so we can go away to a hotel as a couple. It's great, we really enjoy being together, having long walks and quiet dinners. It keeps us together.

Ronnie, father to George, one year old.

I was so jealous of my husband's life. It seemed that while I was sitting breastfeeding he was still able to enjoy his business trips abroad and his weekends of football. For a few weeks I really wondered how we were going to resolve it and I became really depressed. Then I decided to express milk more often and introduce my baby to the odd formula feed and suddenly I was free! Even if I just went out of the house for an hour I felt like myself once more.

Charlie, mother to Ryan, nine months old.

GOING BACK TO WORK

Being a parent is a bit like a rollercoaster ride, but being a working parent offers even more ups and downs! The secret to any working parent's success is organization, and more organization – and unfortunately you have to start it while you are still on maternity leave. It is tempting to forget about work completely in the first two or three months with your baby, but there are some very good reasons for reminding yourself that you will be going back:

To keep your job   In the UK you are required to tell your company, in writing, that you intend to return to work (if you have taken the full 40 weeks of leave that you are entitled to if you have worked there for two years). If you don't, your employer does not have to keep your job open for you. If you have only taken the minimum 14 weeks leave you have an automatic right to return to your job. Make sure you give all the written notification you are required to.

To allow time for sorting out your childcare   Finding a nanny or childminder can take longer than you would imagine, and you don't want to leave your baby in the hands of someone purely because there were no other alternatives at the last minute. Your lifestyle, income and hours of work will probably direct you towards your type of childcare, be it nanny, childminder or nursery – or you may find it better to combine options, such as a childminder and your mother-in-law. You can get a list of registered childminders and nurseries from your local authority and lists of nannies agencies from the phone book, although your best recommendation for any of these is always word of mouth. Make sure you interview or visit each option carefully and don't just consider your baby's immediate needs – as she grows up she will need plenty of stimulation, learning and play opportunities, as well as love.

To make your return easier   By staying in touch with what is happening at work, you will find it easier to slip back into your role when you return. Going back to your job after such a break can be difficult, but it will be especially so if you feel out of touch and unaware of company developments or even the office gossip! Give your colleagues a ring once a month and see if you can be put on a mailing list for anything relevant, especially the parties!

To remind yourself that there is another 'you'   The first few months at home with your baby, although exhausting, are very rewarding. Here is someone who loves you unconditionally – and there is nothing better in the world. As you become used to your routine with your baby and begin to make friends and contacts in the community, it can become harder and harder to imagine going back to work – especially if you haven't spoken to anyone there since the day you left. Keeping in touch with work will help to remind you of your other side – the woman who gets a buzz out of her job when it's going well, the woman who enjoys the social aspect of her work and the woman who has something other than babies to discuss with her partner at the end of the day. If you are looking forward to being that person again it will be easier to wave goodbye to your baby and view the end of your maternity leave positively.

To help you decide whether or not you want to return　If you are uncertain, staying in touch may help to swing you either way. If, on talking to colleagues, you just feel that you are glad to be out of it all, then perhaps you should be doing some sums to see if a career break would be possible financially. Remember to consider the following before you decide:

✿ Would you be able to pick up your career in, say, five years time?
✿ How would you feel about being financially dependent on your partner?
✿ Do you have a company pension that would be affected?
✿ Could you work part-time or from home, instead of giving up work completely?

As a single parent without a car and working long hours it was impossible to find a childminder that could fit around me, and who I liked. I ended up having a nanny which was more affordable than I thought, and meant that someone was there for Lucy if I was delayed. Also having her come to my flat was so much easier in the mornings.

Jayne, mother to Lucy, eight months old.

YOUR FIRST WEEK BACK

Plan for your first week back in advance by making sure that your baby is taking a bottle some weeks before, and that you are able to express proficiently, if that's what you intend to do. You may want to express milk for every feed while you are at work or you may find it easier to offer your baby formula milk for those feeds (see Combining breast and bottle, page 84).

A few days before you go back, try a dry run at getting up and out in the morning in order to arrive in time for work. Practise dropping your baby off at nursery at the allotted time and so on. It will help you feel much more confident and in control on the day you do actually return.

If possible, arrange to start back at work gradually – perhaps just doing two or three days a week at first. This will help you get into the swing of things and make sure your childcare is working satisfactorily. Ideally you should arrange this before you leave for maternity leave so that your employers know where they stand.

Don't feel you have to forget you have children completely. It is natural to mention your baby and even to have a photograph on your desk, but don't talk about how much you are missing her to the extent that your boss wonders how long you will stick the job.

I always thought that my company could not survive without me (and I think they did too), so while I was on maternity leave I asked them to send me the memos of important meetings and so on. I soon realized that there were plenty of people who were happy to jump into my shoes. It also made me realize how uninterested I'd become in the whole business since having Florence. I decided to stay at home with her in the end, which I never thought I would do originally.

Claire, mother to Florence, seven months old.

I always make the bottles and pack up the bag for Molly the night before so that in the morning I only have myself to get ready. I also set my alarm so that I wake up before she does – it's the only way I can get a shower in peace.

Krina, mother to Molly, ten months old.

I want to work part-time from home, but I was wondering whether I could get away with not having any childcare and working while the baby sleeps.

Yvonne, mother to Katy, eight weeks old.

You might be able to, but on the days when she doesn't sleep for long you will find yourself working in the evenings and weekends, which is certain to eventually have an adverse effect on your relationship with your partner, and maybe your baby. You don't want to spend all the time you are with her wishing that she would sleep for longer, do you? The other problem is that a child's sleeping pattern inevitably changes and is unreliable so you will not be able to set aside a specific number of hours each day for a period of months. All things considered it is probably wiser to accept that you will have to pay a certain amount in childcare per week. Remember that, by working at home, you are making substantial savings on travel, lunches etc. anyway.

As a new Dad I'm beginning to resent the number of hours that I'm away from home each day. I never get in until 8pm when Keir is just going to bed and I leave quite early in the morning. I'm worried that he will never love me in the same way he loves his mum, or even worse, his childminder.

Ewan, father to Keir, six months old.

Every working parent worries about the amount of time that they spend away from their child, but there is no reason why that should have a detrimental effect on your relationship with him – especially as you are so aware of it and obviously keen to work at it. These points should help you come to terms with your situation:

- ✿ Like everyone else, your son can love more than one person at once and, if he does love his carer, you should be pleased that he is happy, secure and confident in her care.
- ✿ When you are at home, forget work entirely and dedicate yourself to family life.
- ✿ Make the most of the time you are with your baby by taking over his care and doing bathtime, nappies, etc. Your partner will appreciate it too.
- ✿ Plan ahead to make sure that you book time off work for the important occasions in your son's life.
- ✿ As your son gets older, take up a hobby together and read to him at bedtimes.

MAKING TIME FOR YOURSELF

Whether you are at home with your baby all day or going out to work, you need time to unwind and be yourself instead of being a mother, a lover or an employee the whole time. You will find you perform more happily and efficiently in every one of your many roles as a result.

As soon as you are able to express some milk or offer your baby a bottle of formula milk, allocate time in your diary to hand her over to your partner or a babysitter and just be 'you'. Don't wait until there's a gap in your diary when nothing else is happening, you need to make sure that you get 'me' time regularly, even if it is just an hour or two each week. You don't even have to do anything special – you may want to go and have a long soak in the bath, go to a café with some friends (and no babies!), or go and read a paper in the park.

It is very easy for women to get drawn in all directions until they feel they are pleasing everybody but themselves. Even worse, you may find yourself adopting a tired martyred expression which does nobody any favours – least of all yourself. So get out there, remember what you were like before you had a baby – and have some fun!

USEFUL CONTACTS

Association for Postnatal Illness Provides advice and support for people suffering from postnatal depression

25 Jerdan Place, London SW6 1BE (0171 386 0868)

CRY-SIS Support Group Helpline for parents of babies who cry incessantly and those who have sleep problems

BM CRY-SIS, London WC1N 3XX (0171 404 5011, 8 am to 11 pm)

Day Care Trust Supplies information about childcare, its costs and availability

4 Wild Court, London WC2B 4AU (0171 405 5617)

Gingerbread Support and practical help for one-parent families with a network of self-help groups

16–17 Clerkenwell Close, London EC1R 0AA (0171 336 8184)

La Leche League Provides help and advice for breastfeeding mothers

Box 3424, London, WC1N 3XX (0171 242 1278)

or 12 Wicklow Street, Dublin, Eire (2 +353 (1) 710291)

Maternity Alliance Works for improvements in health care and support for parents-to-be and in the first year of life

45 Beech Street, London EC2P 2LX (0171 588 8582)

Meet-A-Mum Association Support and counselling for women suffering from postnatal depression, feeling lonely or isolated

14 Willis Road, Croydon, Surrey CR0 2XX (0181 665 0357)

National Childbirth Trust (for information about breastfeeding, postnatal support groups and doulas)

Alexandra House, Oldham Terrace, Acton, London W3 6NH (0181 992 8637)

National Council for One Parent Families Campaigns to improve the position of one parent families and offers an information service

255 Kentish Town Road, London NW5 2LX (0171 267 1361)

Parents at Work Offers advice and support for working parents

45 Beech Street, Barbican, London EC2Y 8AD (0171 628 3578)

Relate Runs centres around the UK offering counselling for relationship difficulties

Herbert Gray College, Little Church Street, Rugby,Warwickshire CV21 3AP (01788 573241)

TAMBA (Twins and Multiple Birth Association)

PO Box 30, Little Sutton, South Wirral L66 1TH (0151 348 0020)

USA

International Childbirth Education Association

Minneapolis, USA (612 854 8660)

FURTHER READING

Baby and Child Penelope Leach. Penguin, 1979

The Baby Bible (from pregnancy to prams, from nappies to night feeds, choosing the best for you and your baby) Juliet Leigh. Gollanz, 1996

The Complete Book of Mother & Baby Care. Elizabeth Fenwick. Dorling Kindersley, 1995

The Complete Baby and Child Care Dr Miriam Stoppard. Dorling Kindersley, 1995

Feeding (The simple solution) Hollyer & Smith. Ward Lock, 1997

The Complete Baby & Toddler Meal Planner Annabel Karmel. Ebury Press, 1991

Sleep (The secret of problem-free nights) Hollyer & Smith. Ward Lock, 1996

The Working Parent's Survival Guide Irene Pilia. Ward Lock, 1997

Toddler Taming Dr Christopher Green. Arrow, 1992

Index